**The Effect of Public Policy on
Housing Markets**

The Effect of Public Policy on Housing Markets

Hugh O. Nourse
University of Missouri-St. Louis

Lexington Books
D.C. Heath and Company
Lexington, Massachusetts
Toronto   London

331.833
N93e

Library of Congress Cataloging in Publication Data

Nourse, Hugh O.
    The effect of public policy on housing markets.

    1. Housing—United States. I. Title.
HD7293.N68   301.5'4'0973   73-930
ISBN 0-669-85092-6

FV

Published simultaneously in Canada.

Printed in the United States of America.

International Standard Book Number: 0-669-85092-6

Library of Congress Catalog Card Number: 73-930

Table of Contents

	Preface	vii
Chapter 1	Introduction: Central Themes	1
Chapter 2	The Effect of Public Housing on Property Values in St. Louis	3
Chapter 3	A Regression Method for Real Estate Price Index Construction, with *Martin J. Bailey* and *Richard F. Muth*	15
Chapter 4	Redistribution of Income from Public Housing	29
Chapter 5	Redistribution of Income from the Pruitt-Igoe Public Housing Projects	43
Chapter 6	The Economics of Urban Renewal	51
Chapter 7	The Effect of Air Pollution on House Values	63
Chapter 8	The Effect of a Negative Income Tax on the Number of Substandard Housing Units	75
Chapter 9	The Filtering Process: The Webster Groves and Kankakee Cases, with *Donald Guy*	91

vi

Chapter 10   The Effect of Aging and Income
              Transition on Neighborhood House
              Values, with *Donald Phares* and
              John Stevens   107

Chapter 11   Economic Analysis of Standard
              Quality Housing   121

Index   129

About the Author   131

Preface

Housing policy has been discussed, legislated, administered, and made anew with less economic analysis and statistical testing than most areas of public action. The studies in this volume are an attempt at positive analysis of the impact of public policy on the housing market. Some of the policies analyzed are housing policies, some are not, but all those in the book affect housing prices and quality. It is important for the reader to know that the papers are in chronological order, and were completed over a ten-year period, beginning in 1962 and ending in 1972.

All but three of the studies (Chapters 5, 10, and 11) have been published elsewhere. Furthermore, several of the studies have been co-authored: Chapter 3 with Martin J. Bailey and Richard F. Muth; Chapter 9, with Donald Guy; and Chapter 10, with Donald Phares and John Stevens.

Because these studies were scattered over a ten-year period, they do not include the latest information. Nevertheless, they do represent analysis of the data and events at the time they were written. Cumulatively, they represent a study of the economic impact of alternative public policies on prices and the quality of housing.

The initial inspiration and training on questions of real estate were due to Roy Wenzlick, for whom I worked as an associate editor and economist from 1959 to 1961. Since then I have discussed my research with teachers at the University of Chicago and with colleagues at Washington University, the University of Illinois, and the University of Missouri-St. Louis. A fellowship from the Earhardt Foundation and grants from the Institute for Research on Poverty at the University of Wisconsin, the United States Public Health Service, the Social Science Research Institute at Washington University, and the Department of Housing and Urban Development have made much of the data collection and research in this book possible.

The results, of course, are completely my own responsibility, except in the chapters where co-authorship is noted.

HUGH O. NOURSE

St. Louis, Missouri
December 1972

1

Introduction: Central Themes

Few issues in public policy include more untested conjectures than housing. Policies affecting the demand and supply of housing, and thus its price, include public housing, zoning, urban renewal, welfare payments, building codes, mortgage guarantees, and open occupancy laws. Much has been written on all these topics, but few rigorous empirical studies have surfaced to test the implications of alternative policy proposals. The group of papers in this book are an attempt at just such an appraisal.

The title may imply a broader range of questions than is actually covered. The work of testing a single innocent declaration of fact is time-consuming and often undecisive. The following statements are evaluated within the context of the papers included in this collection:

A public housing project raises assessed values for blocks around it and thus provides a net gain to the city even though the land for public housing was taken off the tax rolls.

Somebody other than the poor must be gaining from public housing.

The urban renewal program removes slums and improves housing.

Air pollution has a detrimental effect on residential property values.

A negative income tax plan can substitute for current public expenditures aiding the poor, such as public housing.

The deterioration of neighborhoods, as expressed through property values, is caused primarily by the age of the neighborhood.

There are two themes central to all of these seemingly unrelated hypotheses. One is the application and development of new methods of measurement and analyses of real estate markets. The emphasis on techniques surfaces in three papers: in Chapter 3, on the regression method for real estate price index construction; Chapter 7, on the effect of air pollution on house values; and Chapter 9, on the filtering process. The first of these papers shows how to construct a real estate price index that attempts to control for the changing quality of housing on the market each year. The second demonstrates the use of a linear programming framework in understanding price determination in the housing market. The third introduces the use of city directory data in analyzing long-run changes in neighborhood income levels.

The second theme developed through all of these papers is an evaluation of alternative strategies for housing the poor. We begin with public housing and find that not all of the benefits expected from it can be documented. Historically, public housing was the first attempt at directly solving the problem

1

of housing the poor through new construction. A related policy was that of urban renewal. Chapters 2, 4, 5, and 6 explore the supposed benefits to be derived from both urban renewal and public housing. The evidence supporting urban renewal turns out to be much slimmer than for public housing. In recent years, the negative income tax has been suggested as an alternative to these subsidies in kind. Chapter 8 attempts to determine whether, indeed, such a plan could substitute for public housing programs.

Policymakers have been trying for years to find ways to stabilize neighborhood property values. Ghetto expansion in inner cities has led to declines in income and eventually abandonment of property by commercial and industrial users as well as residents. A bevy of policy tools, such as the occupancy permit and open occupancy laws, has been implemented in an attempt to stabilize neighborhood property values. They are attempts to stabilize neighborhood community values and are a proxy for social and cultural goals. Policies so constructed are difficult to evaluate because there has been little empirical and analytical work on the process of change actually taking place. Chapter 10 tackles one aspect of this change: the way in which aging and income declines affected values in selected neighborhoods in the St. Louis metropolitan area.

The concluding chapter draws on the evidence presented in the empirical studies and presents the implications of these results for understanding whether there is such a thing as a standard quality housing unit. The hypothesis will be that the standard quality of housing for any economy depends upon the amount of subsidy that the electorate will be willing to contribute to poor families. Indeed, attempts to raise quality by fiat through building codes result in the current crisis of abandoned housing in cities across the nation. These propositions are not tested with empirical evidence, and need to be so tested. Research, however, should not only be for testing hypotheses, but for suggesting new ones as a result of other evidence uncovered.

2

The Effect of Public Housing on Property Values in St. Louis

Note: "I cannot quite agree with you that the cities or the municipalities are without benefits in this matter. One of the principal arguments, with which I go along, is that the establishment of a modern housing project in a city raises the assessed valuation for blocks around it and puts back onto the municipal tax rolls a great deal more money than is taken off by the land that is occupied by these public-housing projects. That has been one of the principal arguments that I have heard through the years from public-housing agencies."—Congressman A.S. Mike Monroney (1948)[1]

The purpose of this study is to determine whether public housing projects tend to raise the values of surrounding properties. Low-income families living in public housing projects receive a substantial housing subsidy, averaging about $115 per month plus utilities.[a] Clearly, the public housing program tends to increase their well-being. Nevertheless, if the welfare of these families were the only concern, they could be made better off by an equivalent income subsidy that they could spend as they wish. Therefore, the justification for the public housing program must be sought in its external effects on the surrounding community. Housing reformers have claimed that "decent housing instead of slums means less crime, less juvenile delinquency, lower costs for police and fire protection; it also means better health, lower death rates, and lower costs of medical care."[2] As Congressman Monroney pointed out in the quotation above, many people believe that public housing projects raise the value of surrounding

Source: Reprinted from LAND ECONOMICS, vol. 39, no. 4 (The University of Wisconsin Press, November 1963).

The author thanks especially Richard F. Muth for his valuable criticisms, suggestions, and encouragement. Margaret G. Reid, Martin J. Bailey, and Roy Wenzlick have also made many valuable suggestions. To the Relm Foundation he is grateful for financial support that enabled him to spend a year with the Urban Economics Workshop at the University of Chicago.

[a]The average gross rent per unit per month (including utilities) during the fiscal year 1956 for public housing units built under the Housing Act of 1949 was $33.55 while the development costs of these units averaged $10,715. (Ibid., p. 188, 190.) Since private, multi-family dwellings typically have monthly rents (excluding utilities) of about one seventy-second of their value, the average public housing unit would rent on the private market for slightly under $150 per month plus utilities. Therefore, the subsidy provided the family living in a public housing project averages about $115 plus the value of utilities provided.

properties. To my knowledge, however, the effect of public housing projects on surrounding property values have received almost no study.[b]

The change in the site value of the neighborhood in which a public housing project is built is one measure of part of the net social return necessary to justify construction of the project. Site value is the value of a particular plot of land if cleared of buildings and other improvements.[3] It is the present value of the net income that can be earned by investing in the improvements necessary to put the land to its optimal use. In most cases the improvements of the environment that add to the land value of a site are public value or rent.[c] Thus, in the case of public housing, we can measure one way in which the construction of the project improves or degrades the environment by measuring the change in the land values of the neighborhood.

Although site values represent the economic value of location, I will have to use the value of land plus improvements in this study. The areas with which I am dealing do not have enough vacant land. Less than 10 percent of the land is vacant. The only prices available except for vacant land sales are those for land and improvements. This will add to the complexity of analyzing changes in the prices over time. Changes in the improvements, other than depreciation, may increase the property value without any change in the land values. The two major influences on the price index used, other than changes in land values, will be depreciation of the improvements and inflation. Inflation will be taken into account by deflating by a building cost index. Depreciation on the improvements, however, will tend to make increases in market prices less than increases in land values, or will tend to make decreases in market prices greater than decreases in land values. Although changes in land values in one neighborhood may be underestimated, a comparison of the index of property values between

[b]The only attempt to measure the effect of public housing on surrounding property values of which I am aware was made by Leo Grebler in his book, HOUSING MARKET BEHAVIOR IN A DECLINING AREA (New York, New York: Columbia University Press, 1953), pp. 90-93. He compared changes in assessed value in an area of influence of three blocks abutting Stuyvesant Town and three blocks abutting Jacob Riis Houses in New York City with changes in assessed value in the whole Lower East Side which included the housing projects. He found that the blocks abutting the housing projects had greater increases in assessed value than the total for the Lower East Side. The main criticism of this study is that total assessed value for an area may change because of a change in the proportion of tax exempt properties or because of demolitions. Therefore, the blocks abutting public housing may have greater percentage increases in total assessments than the Lower East Side because a lower percentage of properties became tax exempt or were demolished in the abutting blocks than in the whole area. Likewise, total assessments might have increased more rapidly in the abutting block if the tax assessors mistakenly believed that the projects had raised surrounding property values or for reasons unrelated to public housing.

[c]There are exceptions, however, when an entrepreneur deliberately invests capital to raise land value. For example, a developer may buy agricultural land and then pave streets and put in sewers and water mains in order to raise the land value. In such cases parts of the increased income must not be capitalized as rent but as the return on capital invested in improvements.

two neighborhoods does not distort the comparison of the underlying change in land values, if we assume that depreciation affects the indexes in both neighborhoods equally.

Two additional problems should be considered. The first is that the property value may decline greatly on the second sale because of economic obsolescence while the land values have increased. In fact, the increased land values may cause buildings to become uneconomic if they do not furnish enough return to cover the rent of the land. A particular example of the above problem would be the sale of a tenement, whose best use would be a parking lot. The buyer will have to tear down the building. In this case the building has no value or even negative value. The second problem is that the slum properties are quite often small plots. They are too small for industrial or commerical use and if a speculator bought up several contiguous parcels and tore down the buildings he would enhance the value of the land. Thus, part of the increase in value represents return on his investment and is not due to any public improvements such as public housing. These problems would be important for this study only if they influenced one area more than its comparative area. One such comparison will be discussed later.

The method used in this study is to define control areas as similar as possible to public housing neighborhoods and to compare the trend in property values in each. Three major problems need to be solved: first, there is the problem of determining the public housing and the control neighborhoods; second, real estate sales prices must be obtained; and third, a way must be found to index the sales prices to measure the price trend. Each of these problems is taken up in turn in the succeeding sections.

Delimitation of the Public Housing and Control Neighborhoods

The main problem in defining the neighborhoods is to find areas that were comparable to the public housing neighborhoods before the projects were built and that have developed in much the same way. It would be ideal if each public housing neighborhood and its control neighborhood had been exactly alike in all characteristics that influence property values before construction of the projects and had developed in the same way with the sole exception of the construction of the housing projects. This, of course, is impossible. Therefore, differences are analyzed to see how they might influence price trend comparisons.

The eight St. Louis public housing projects in my study are arranged into three neighborhoods. The public housing neighborhood is defined as the area surrounding each project area, about two to three blocks wide. No fewer blocks were defined within the neighborhoods to insure availability of enough sales for an index. On the other hand, a greater area was not defined because the influence of public housing would weaken as distance from the projects increased. There are practical reasons, too, in that railroad yards are just two blocks north of projects 1-2 and 1-7, Lafayette Park is three blocks west of project 1-2, and the downtown district is four blocks south of project 1-3. In outlining these neighborhoods projects 1-4, 1-5, 1-6, and 1-1 are all in one neighborhood, hereafter called area A. Projects 1-2 and 1-7 are in one neighborhood, area B, and projects 1-3 and Neighborhood Gardens are in one neighborhood, area C. The locations of these areas are as follows: (A) Madison Street and Cass Avenue on the north, Leffingwell and Jefferson Avenues on the west, Franklin and Lucas Avenues on the south, and 12th Street on the east; (B) Gratiot Street on the north, 21st Street, Mississippi Avenue, and Dolman Street on the west, Lafayette Avenue, Geyer Avenue, and Park Avenue on the south, and 10th and 8th Streets on the east; and (C) Mullanphy Street on the north, 11th Street on the west, Franklin Avenue on the south, and Broadway on the east.

The three control neighborhoods have been selected on the basis of average contract monthly rents, land use, population, and other data as well as on my personal knowledge of the area. The first step in selecting the control areas was to locate the census tracts in St. Louis that had average contract monthly rents in 1940 comparable to those in the census tracts where public housing projects were eventually to be located. Then on the basis of personal knowledge of the area, discussions with appraisers, and average contract rent per unit in each block as recorded in the *1940 Census Block Statistics* specific areas were outlined. These were adjusted to make land use in the control areas more nearly comparable to the public housing areas.

These areas were bounded as follows: (A₁) (The subscript ₁ shows that the area is the control neighborhood for public housing neighborhood A.) Chouteau Avenue and Papin Street on the north, Ewing Avenue and Grand Boulevard on the west, Caroline Street, Rutger Street, and Hickory Street on the south, and Jefferson Avenue and Missouri Avenue on the east; (B₁) North Market Street on the north, 13th Street on the west, Tyler Street and Brooklyn Street on the south, and Second Street on the east; (C₁) Russell Boulevard and Carroll Street on the north, Third Street and Menard Street on the west, Victor Street on the south, and Kosciusko Street on the east.

To compare these neighborhoods, data on the following characteristics were obtained from the 1940, 1950, and 1960 Census: total dwelling units, percent of units occupied, percent of occupied units tenant-occupied, percent of occupied units occupied by nonwhite persons, percent of units built prior to 1900 (1940 only), percent of units built in 1900 through 1919 (1940 only), percent of units with all plumbing facilities, percent of units with more than 1.5 persons per room (1940 and 1950), and with more than 1 person per room (1960); average contract rent per unit per month, income of families and unrelated individuals (1949 only), employment status of males (1940 and 1950), and occupation of males (1940 and 1950). Land use data for 1952-1956 in each public housing neighborhood were compared with those of its control neighborhood. Maps of public transportation routes, published by the Public Service Company, show that from 1940 to 1951 no change took place in routes except for a few changeovers from street-car routes to bus routes. If we assume that the Central Business District is bounded by Franklin Avenue on the north, 12th Street on the west, Clark Avenue on the south, and Broadway on the east, then none of the public housing or control neighborhoods is more than 15 minutes from the Central Business District by public transportation.

Most of these characteristics in the control neighborhoods are comparable to those of the public housing neighborhoods. There are some differences at one point in time but these may be unimportant in a comparison of change in property prices over time. The change in the relative differences in each characteristic over time is more important for comparing price trends.[d] These exceptions to the comparability of the public housing and control neighborhoods are now taken up in detail.

Area A_1 showed a greater increase in the proportion of nonwhite occupancy than area A between 1950 and 1960. Nonwhite persons occupied 69 percent of the units in area A_1 in 1940 and 92 percent of the units in area A_1 in 1960; while in area A they occupied 61 percent of the units in 1940 and 75 percent of the units in 1960. This should not have a differential effect on real estate prices in the two neighborhoods as the initial impact of the nonwhite occupancy had been prior to 1940. Of course, one could argue that a housing shortage for nonwhite occupancy would cause higher rents and prices for nonwhites for comparable housing. Therefore, prices and rents may increase more between 1950 and 1960 in area A_1 than area A since the proportion of units occupied by nonwhite persons increased more in the former.

From 1940 to 1960 demolitions and conversions caused a greater percentage reduction of dwelling units in area B than in area B_1, and in area C than in area C_1. From 1940 to 1960 there was a loss of 24 percent of the units in area A, a loss of 23 percent in area A_1, a loss of 46 percent in area B, a loss of 20 percent in area B_1, a loss of 58 percent in area C, and a loss of 38 percent in area C_1. The effect of the differences in the percentage loss of dwelling units between B and B_1, and between C and C_1 on property value comparisons will depend upon the use to which the properties are changed. Some information on this is developed later from the market price data.

_____

[d]This point is pertinent to two of the comparisons. There is a sharp difference in 1940 in the proportion of units occupied by nonwhite persons between area C and C_1, but the difference has remained the same from 1940 through 1960. The comparison of land use reveals differences in use between areas B and B_1 and areas C and C_1. These contrasts might signify differences in land value between two neighborhoods at one point in time but, in a comparison of change in property prices, only changes in use should significantly influence the comparison. Although some evidence turns up later from the market price data, I was unable to get a land use study for a different time period for direct comparison.

General improvements in transportation have affected all of these neighborhoods equally. The timing of one new highway, however, may distort comparisons of price trends in area B with those of area B_1. The highway runs through the middle of area B_1 and the edge of area B. It was constructed first in area B. The land was purchased for this highway in 1949 in area B, and in 1955-56 in area B_1.[4] To the extent that routes were known in advance and that anticipations were that condemnation awards would be higher than market prices, real estate sales prices would increase faster in the speculative area, area B, prior to 1949, and area B_1 prior to 1955-56, than in the comparable area at that time. Of course, an anticipation that condemnation awards would be low would depress the markets concerned.

Construction of the Real Estate Price Indexes

Real estate selling prices were estimated as the upper limit of the $500 range indicated by the amount of tax stamps on sales recorded in the Real Estate Abstract of the Assessor's Office of the City of St. Louis. Although the actual sales price of a real estate transfer is not recorded, federal tax stamps must be affixed to the deed in an amount not less than $0.55 per $500 of value conveyed, or part thereof.[5] There is no law against putting on more stamps than necessary, so that this source will tend to give overestimates of the market price. This can be disregarded if the bias is assumed to be reasonably constant over time. A further complication is that the sales prices estimated from the tax stamps do not always indicate the whole price paid for a property. These estimates may cover only a partial interest in the property; they may cover the transfer of more than one property; and they may cover only the equity conveyed and not a mortgage assumed by the buyer. If the transaction was only a partial interest, the sales price, which was estimated from tax stamps, was multiplied by the inverse of the fractional interest in the property transferred. If the mortgage debt outstanding assumed by the buyer was stated in the deed, its value was added to the sales price indicated by the tax stamps. The sale was removed from the study if the outstanding mortgage debt assumed by the buyer was not stated in the deed. The sale was also discarded if the value indicated by the tax stamps represented the value of more than one property transferred, unless all of the properties were in the same study area and all the properties were sold as a unit in at least two different years.

In fact, only sales with a previous sale on the same property were used to compute the price index in each of the six neighborhoods. Although this means that many sales prices were unused, the index will not be subject to annual variation because of changes in the quality and kind of property in the market each year. If no major changes are made in the improvements between sales, the changes in the index will show the changes in property value over time. A sample study of building permits, which is described in detail later, indicates that improvements added between sales were insignificant in these neighborhoods.

From these data percentage relatives were computed for each property. Prices within any one year were averaged to obtain a sales estimate for that year for the property. For example, if the property sold in 1941 and 1955, at an indicated price of $2,000 in 1941, and an average of $5,000 in 1955, the price relatives for this property would be 1.00 in 1941 and 2.50 in 1955. Since the index computations require geometric means, these relatives were converted to logarithms.

A new index method, first used in this study, is to link the relatives of the sales on each property by means of a regression equation.[6] The superiority of this method over others is that it is the minimum variance estimator of the true index on the usual assumptions about residuals in the method of least squares. Since the price relative of a final sale is the ratio of the final sale to the initial sale, we can consider the logarithm of the price relative to be equal to the logarithm of the true but unknown index for the final year less the logarithm of the true but unknown index for the initial year plus a random variable. The computation of the index in each neighborhood can then be treated as a regression problem using the following equation:

$$\log \frac{P_f}{P_0} = \sum_{j=1}^{j=T} (\log I_j) X_j + \log U.$$

In this equation X_j is equal to -1 in the year of the initial sale, 1 in the year of resale, and 0 otherwise. The coefficients of the X_j, the $\log I_j$, are the terms to be estimated, and are the logarithms of the real estate price index for year j. The logarithm of U is a random variable; P_f is the sales price in the final year; and P_0 is the initial sales price for any pair of sales on a property.

Since the indexes in all of the areas must run twenty-two or twenty-three years, and the logarithm of the price relative of the first year is zero, the computational problem is estimating the coefficients of a regression equation with twenty-one or twenty-two independent variables. The computer available to me could not handle this as a regression problem. Fortunately, the matrix necessary to solve the problem is easily calculated. It is no more than a square matrix with as many columns as independent variables. Each diagonal element is the sum of all the initial and final sales each year. The off-diagonal elements are minus the number of final sales each year with an initial sale in the year of the row. This matrix is then inverted and multiplied times a column vector. The elements of the column are minus the sum of all relatives of final sales with an initial sale in the year of the given row plus the sum of all relatives of final sales with initial sales in years previous to the given row. The products are the logarithms of the index. The computer could handle this matrix algebra. It turns out that this method makes each yearly index a weighted average of all sales.

Table 2-1 lists the indexes for each neighborhood as computed by the above regression method. These indexes were calculated from 5044 initial and final sales, which were divided among the areas in the following way: area A 1512; area A_1 634; area B 1702; area B_1 328; area C 250; area C_1 618.

In order to avoid the possibility of basing the indexes on one year that was unusual (1937), the indexes for each neighborhood were rebased on the average of 1937 through 1939, the years prior to the establishment of the St. Louis Housing Authority. The influence of the general price trend was removed by dividing each series by a building cost index.[e]

It appears that there is no difference in the trend of prices in areas A and A_1, and B and B_1, and that the trend of prices is higher in area C than in area C_1. Therefore, if we assume that the only differences in neighborhood growth between the public housing and control neighborhoods was the construction of the public housing projects, public housing had no effect on property values in area A, nor area B, and a positive effect on property values in area C. A two-tail statistical test of significance of the ratio of each public housing area index

Table 2-1. Real Estate Selling Price Indexes, Constant Dollars (1937-39 = 1.00)

Year	Area A	Area A_1	Area B	Area B_1	Area C	Area C_1
1937	1.018	.9962	1.000	1.061	.6642	1.105
1938	1.114	1.154	1.106	1.282	1.438	1.042
1939	1.043	1.029	1.069	.8695	1.238	1.027
1940	1.092	.9279	1.130	1.383	1.688	1.339
1941	.9937	1.248	1.311	1.572	1.308	.8233
1942	1.204	1.042	1.175	1.683	1.186	1.147
1943	1.323	1.051	1.254	1.336	.9820	1.248
1944	1.275	1.393	1.558	1.075	1.442	1.109
1945	1.344	1.146	1.427	1.512	1.246	.966
1946	1.390	1.353	1.550	1.486	1.362	1.260
1947	1.271	1.377	1.455	1.559	1.365	1.267
1948	1.275	1.266	1.578	1.818	1.260	1.067
1949	1.045	1.284	1.538	1.656	1.755	1.205
1950	1.301	1.312	1.424	1.990	1.473	1.165
1951	1.225	1.114	1.509	1.529	1.699	1.316
1952	1.233	1.283	1.852	2.131	1.941	1.327
1953	1.205	1.546	1.534	2.340	1.884	1.394
1954	1.169	1.293	1.596	1.743	1.751	1.162
1955	1.222	1.301	1.389	1.813	1.562	1.455
1956	1.302	.9891	1.407	1.787	1.860	1.172
1957	1.135	.8236	1.333	1.021	1.773	1.321
1958	1.123	.8576	1.398	1.492	1.635	1.032
1959	.8916	1.279	1.230	2.373	—	1.006

[e]The building cost index (1937 = 1.00) was calculated from the cost of constructing a standard six-room brick house in St. Louis, as estimated by Roy Wenzlick Research Corporation. These figures are published from time to time in THE REAL ESTATE ANALYST. They are based on current wage rates and material costs and the actual labor time and amounts of material used to build such a house in the 1930s. Although no account is taken of changes in labor efficiency, new materials or equipment are substituted as they come in common use. Only current figures are published. The unpublished master set of figures was used with the permission of Roy Wenzlick Research Corporation.

number to its comparative index number each year, however, reveals that only one ratio (area B in 1959) is different from one at a confidence level of 95 percent. The data, therefore, do not contradict an hypothesis that public housing has no effect on property values.

Two factors may have accounted for different price trends or in comparable price trends when in fact they were different: more improvements may have been made to buildings between sales in one neighborhood than in another; or some other influence may have been operating in one area that was not in the comparative area. In particular, as pointed out previously, one area may have been changing in the proportion of land devoted to a new use.

There is no significant difference in the value of improvements added between sales between the public housing and control neighborhoods so that there is no change indicated in the price trends from this source. In order to estimate the effect of changes in the improvements between pairs of sales on the same property, building permits and their values for a sample of 96 pairs of sales used in the real estate price indexes were analyzed. Sixteen pairs of sales were taken randomly from each neighborhood. Final sales and the value of the improvements listed on the building permit were deflated by the same building cost index used to deflate the real estate price indexes. The values of improvement changes were depreciated at 2 percent per year to arrive at an estimate of the depreciated constant dollar value of the improvements at the time of the second sale. The percent of the second sale attributable to the change in improvements was estimated by dividing the depreciated and deflated value of the improvement by the deflated value of the second sale. For the total sample the mean was 1.17 percent. To test for any difference between the public housing and control neighborhoods the sample was divided into two equal groups: one for the public housing areas; one for the control areas. Added improvements represented 1.535 percent of the second sale value in public housing neighborhoods and 0.809 percent of the second sale in the control neighborhoods. This difference was not significant at the 5 percent level, is quantitatively unimportant and, if anything, indicates that the estimated price indexes described above tend to overestimate the trend of real estate values in public housing areas relative to their control areas. The value of improvements as indicated by building permits may seriously underestimate their true value but such permits are the only source available.

Another influence may be responsible for the higher trend of prices in area C than in area C_1. It is interesting to note that 14 of the 125 pairs of sales in area C involved truck companies. These are the obvious transactions where one party was a company with *trucking* or *transfer* in the title. It may be an undercount since other property may have been purchased by an individual and leased to a trucking company, or the property may be owned by the individual running a trucking business on the site. There were no trucking companies involved in real estate sales in area C_1. Area A with 2 such sales out of 756 pairs of sales and area

B with 5 such sales out of 851 pairs of sales were the only other areas with trucking transactions in the study. While the sales in area A and C were final sales to truckers those in area B were not. The truckers sold their property in area B in 1946, 1948, and 1954. Of the 14 sales involving truckers in area C, 12 were final purchases. In 9 of the 12 transactions truckers paid a greater increase in price over the previous sale than was shown by the index for area C. For the most part these sales took place between 1950 and 1958. It is therefore quite possible that the truckers' demand for property in area C rather than public housing caused the greater increases in prices in that area over area C_1 in the 1950's. There was a counter demand in area C_1 but it expended its force primarily in 1940 and 1946. Monsanto Chemical Company, owning a great deal of land near the river adjacent to area C_1, began expanding. Of the 309 pairs of sales in area C_1, 9 included purchases by Monsanto. In every case they paid a greater price increase over the previous sale than was indicated by the price index for area C_1. All but two of these sales took place in 1940 and 1946. The others were in 1951 and 1959. The sales prior to 1953 were before public housing project 1-3 was constructed in area C and seem to have kept sales prices in area C_1 from falling further below those of area C.

Conclusions

This study provides no support for the view that public housing projects increase the value of surrounding properties. Property values in area A and B had the same general trend as those in their control neighborhoods. Property values in area C rose somewhat more than those in its control neighborhood although there is some evidence that the increase in prices in area C was at least partly due to truckers' demand. In only one year was there a statistically significant difference between the real estate price indexes of a public housing neighborhood and its control area and in this instance the index for the public housing neighborhood was below that of its control neighborhood.

Of course, the evidence is not conclusive. In the first place only public housing projects in St. Louis were studied. Other projects in other areas with different circumstances might reveal different results. Secondly, real estate prices have been treated as if the price trends were the same regardless of land use. It would have been interesting to analyze properties separately by use. The data, however, were not available for such an analysis. Finally, one can never be certain that the control area is exactly like the study area in all relevant characteristics.

Nevertheless, to my knowledge this is the first detailed study of public housing and property value yet attempted.

Notes

1. House Banking and Currency Committee, HEARINGS, GENERAL HOUSING, 1948, p. 247, quoted in Robert Moore Fisher, TWENTY YEARS OF PUBLIC HOUSING (New York, New York: Harper & Brothers, 1959), p. 195.

2. Dillon S. Myer, Commissioner of the Federal Public Housing Authority, at the HEARINGS before the Committee on Banking and Currency, United States Senate, 80th Congress, on S866 (Washington, D.C., Government Printing Office, 1947), p. 118, quoted in John P. Dean, "The Myths of Housing Reform," AMERICAN SOCIOLOGICAL REVIEW (April 1949), p. 283. For a criticism see the same article, pp. 281-288. In addition, preliminary findings of a recent study by Daniel M. Wilner, Rosabelle Price Walkley, Marvin N. Glasser and Mathew Tayback, "The Effect of Housing Quality on Morbidity," Preliminary Finding of the Johns Hopkins Longitudinal Study, AMERICAN JOURNAL OF PUBLIC HEALTH (December 1958), pp. 1607-1615, found that there is no difference in the morbidity rates of public housing and slum dwellers, once account is taken of the effects of administrative selection among applicants for public housing.

3. For a discussion of the determinants of urban site value see Alfred Marshall, PRINCIPLES OF ECONOMICS, 8th ed. (New York, New York: The Macmillan Company, 1920), Book V, Chapter 11; Richard M. Hurd, PRINCIPLES OF CITY LAND VALUES (New York, New York: Record and Guide, 1924); and Ralph Turvey, THE ECONOMICS OF REAL PROPERTY (London, England: George Allen and Unwin, Ltd., 1957).

4. The Real Estate Abstract maintained by the City of St. Louis Assessor's Office.

5. UNITED STATES STATUTES AT LARGE, XLVII, Part III, 275 (1932); UNITED STATES STATUTES AT LARGE, LIV, 522 (1940); UNITED STATES STATUTES AT LARGE, LV, Part II, 706-707 (1941), cited in Robert L. Tonty, Jeppe Kristensen, and C. Curtis Cable, Jr., "Reliability of Deed Samples as Indicators of Land Market Activity," LAND ECONOMICS (February 1954), p. 47.

6. For a detailed explanation see Martin J. Bailey, Richard F. Muth, and Hugh O. Nourse, "A Regression Method for Real Estate Price Index Construction," JOURNAL OF THE AMERICAN STATISTICAL ASSOCIATION 58 (December, 1963): 993-1010 or Hugh O. Nourse, "The Effect of Public Housing on Property Values in St. Louis" (unpublished Ph.D. dissertation, Department of Economics, University of Chicago, 1962).

3

A Regression Method for Real Estate Price Index Construction
(With Martin J. Bailey and
Richard F. Muth)

Quality differences make estimation of price indexes for real properties difficult, but these can be largely avoided by basing an index on sales prices of the same property at different times. The problem of combining price relatives of repeat sales of properties to obtain a price index can be converted into a regression problem, and standard techniques of regression analysis can be used to estimate the index. This method of estimation is more efficient than others for combining price relatives in that it utilizes information about the price index for earlier periods contained in sales prices in later periods. Standard errors of the estimated index numbers can be readily computed using the regression method, and it permits certain effects on the value of real properties to be eliminated from the index.

1. Introduction

Index numbers of the prices of real properties are difficult to construct. The major problem appears to be the great variation in quality among properties. Thus, indexes based upon the average sales prices of all properties of some particular kind sold in a given period, as in Laurenti,[2] are likely to be deficient in two respects. First, variation in the quality of properties sold from period to period will cause the index to vary more widely than the value of any given property. Second, if there is a progressive change in the quality of properties sold at different times, the index will be biased over time.

One way to avoid these difficulties is to eliminate quality differences using regression analysis. The regression approach has been applied to automobiles by Griliches[1] and to single-family houses by Pendleton,[4]a and Bailey is currently using this approach in a study of prices of single-family houses in the Hyde Park area of Chicago. In this method, one introduces variables measuring important qualitative characteristics along with period effects into a regression analysis of sales prices. Dummy variables[5] are used to describe attributes such as brick construction or corner lot. Dummy variables are also used for period effects so that the data determine the specific functional form of the time index. Coefficients of the period effects yield a multiplicative price index if sales prices are expressed in logarithms. Such a method yields information on the influence

Reprinted from the JOURNAL OF THE AMERICAN STATISTICAL ASSOCIATION, 58 (December 1963): 993-1010.

aA referee of this paper has informed us that the Statistical Division of the Department of Commerce is using this method to evaluate a Laspeyre index for the price of housing.

15

of variation in quality characteristics on sales prices as well as a real estate price index. It also avoids the problem of selecting items of the same quality for comparison at different times. But, where quality characteristics are numerous and difficult to measure, as with multi-family residential and nonresidential properties and with all properties in the older parts of cities, the method may not yield useful results.

Most of the difficulties of specifying and measuring the numerous quality characteristics of real properties can be avoided by basing a price index on sales prices of the same properties at different times. The principal problem in so doing is the fact any given property is sold only at infrequent intervals. Somehow, a means must be found to combine price relatives based upon repeat sales of given properties into a single index. One way of doing so to obtain a multiplicative chain index, which has been employed with various modifications by Wenzlick[7] and Wyngarden,[8] is as follows. First, the price relatives of all properties initially sold in period zero or the base period and resold in the first period are computed, and their geometric mean is taken as the index for the first period. The price relatives for all pairs of transactions for which the first period is that of initial sale are then adjusted or multiplied by the index for the first period. The price index for period two is the geometric mean of all adjusted price relatives with final sale in period two, where the adjustment factor for those price relatives with initial sale in period zero is unity (see equation (7), section 3). The process is then repeated, adjusting all price relatives by multiplying by the index for the period of initial sale and taking the geometric mean of all adjusted price relatives with final sale in a particular period as the index for that period.

The chain method just discussed is computationally simple, though perhaps tedious. But it is inefficient in that it neglects information about the index for earlier periods contained in price relatives with final sales in later periods. Furthermore, computation of the standard errors of the estimated index numbers can be quite difficult, and it is hard to estimate the effects of other changes affecting values of a particular property simultaneously with the index number. In this paper we shall discuss a regression method for combining price relatives based upon repeat sales prices of given properties which avoids the above noted difficulties.

2. Regression Analysis of Repeat Sales Prices

The model upon which our regression method is based is as follows. Let:

$$R_{itt'} = \frac{B_{t'}}{B_t} \times U_{itt'}, \quad \text{or} \tag{1}$$

$$r_{itt'} = -b_t + b_{t'} + u_{itt'},$$

where lower case letters stand for the logarithms of the corresponding capital letters. $R_{itt'}$ is the ratio of the final sales price in period t' to initial sales price in period t for the ith pair of transactions with initial and final sales in these two periods. B_t and $B_{t'}$ are the true but unknown indexes for period t and t', respectively, where $t = 0, 1, \ldots, T-1$, and $t'=1, \ldots, T$. While other assumptions are possible, we shall assume for now that the residuals in log form, $u_{itt'}$, have zero means, the same variances σ^2, and are uncorrelated with each other. In section 4 we shall explore the problem of correlated residuals.

Estimation of the unknown B's may be treated as a regression problem. Let x_t take the value -1 if period t is the period of initial sale, $+1$ if the period of final sale, and 0 otherwise for each pair of transactions. To normalize the index, let $B_0=1$ or $b_0=0$.[b] Using the above conventions, equation (1) becomes:

$$r_{itt'} = \sum_{j=1}^{T} b_j x_j + u_{itt'},$$

or, in matrix notation:

$$r = xb + u. \tag{2}$$

In (2) r and u are n-dimensional column vectors, where $n = \sum_{t,t'} n_{tt'}$, $n_{tt'}$ being the number of pairs of transactions with initial sale in period t and final sale in t'; b is a T-dimensional column vector of unknown logarithms of the index numbers to be estimated; and x is an $n \times T$ matrix. For a pair of transactions whose initial period of sale is other than the base period, i.e., $t=1, \cdots, T-1$, the corresponding row of x has a -1 in the tth column; for any pair the corresponding row has a $+1$ in the t'th column; all other elements of x are zeros.

Given the assumptions made above about u, the least-squares estimator:

$$\hat{b} = (x'x)^{-1}(x'r), \tag{3}$$

is the minimum variance linear unbiased estimator of b. The tth diagonal element of $(x'x)$, which is a $T \times T$ matrix, is simply the number of pairs of transactions with initial sale in period t plus the number of pairs with final sale

---

[b]Alternatively, we could have expressed the model in terms of period-to-period changes in the index number. To do so, let c_j, $j = 1, \ldots, T$, be the log of the relative change in the index from period $j - 1$ period to j and x_j equal $+1$ if the period $j-1$ to j is included in the interval between initial and final sale and 0 otherwise. It can be shown that the two forms of the model yield identical estimates of the index number for any period. The ratio of the index estimated by the method discussed in the text for any pair of periods is thus independent of the base period selected. This follows because the ratio of the estimated indexes for period t' to period t is merely the product of the estimated period-to-period changes from t to t'. We prefer the form of the model discussed in the text, however, because it is computationally simpler.

in period t. The t, t'th off-diagonal element of $(x'x)$ is $-n_{tt'}$. Finally, $(x'r)$ is a T-dimensional vector whose tth element is the sum of all price relatives for which period t is the period of final sale less the sum of all those for which t is the period of initial sale.

One advantage of the regression method is that it can be easily modified to eliminate the effects on value of certain changes in a property between the periods of initial and final sale. Examples of such changes are remodeling of or addition to a structure, a change in the number of dwelling units in an apartment building, a change in the race of the residents of a building or a neighborhood, and sale for demolition and redevelopment of the property to a new use. Using p appropriate variables to describe changes in a property which affect its value, the regression equation to be estimated becomes

$$R_{itt'} = \frac{B_{t'}}{B_t} X_{T+1}^{b_{T+1}} \cdots X_{T+p}^{b_{T+p}} U_{itt'},$$

or, in log form,

$$r_{itt'} = \sum_{j=1}^{T+p} b_j x_j + u_{itt'}. \tag{4}$$

The element in the tth row and t'th column of $(x'x)$, $t = 1, \ldots, T, t' = T + 1,$ $\ldots, T + p$, is simply the sum of all values of $x_{t'}$ for which the period t is the period of final sale less the sum of all $x_{t'}$ for which t is the period of initial sale. For $t, t' = T + 1, \ldots, T + p$, of course, the element of $(x'x)$ is the sum of the cross products over all observations, $\sum x_t x_{t'}$, while the last p elements of $(x'x)$ are of the form $\sum_n x_t r$.

For some purposes one might want to adjust the price index for depreciation. Unfortunately, a depreciation adjustment cannot be readily estimated along with the price index using our regression method. Assuming that properties depreciate at a constant rate per unit time, our model would become

$$R_{itt'} = \frac{B_{t'}}{B_t} e^{-c(t'-t)} U_{itt'}, \quad \text{or}$$

$$r_{itt'} = \sum_{j=1}^{T+1} b_j x_j + u_{itt'}, \tag{5}$$

where $x_{T+1} = (t'-t)$, the number of periods from initial to final sale, and $b_{T+1} = -c$, the negative of the rate of depreciation. But the vector of values of x_{T+1} can be obtained by multiplying the matrix x in (2) by the column vector whose transpose is $(1, 2, \ldots, T)$. Hence, the x matrix in (5) is singular. In applying our method, therefore, additional information would be needed in order to adjust the price index for depreciation.

The method described above has another characteristic which some may feel is a disadvantage. If the regression method were to be used to construct an index on a continuing basis, each time another period would be added to the index the whole regression would have to be re-estimated. Doing so would make most efficient use of the available data, since sales in any given period add to the information available about the index in all earlier periods. The additional computations would not be much of a burden if a computer could be used. But it might prove irksome continually to revise the index for earlier periods, particularly if the index is published and widely used.

Continual revision of the index could be avoided, however, by recomputing the regression in order to obtain the best estimate of the index for the latest period only. This period is the one of greatest practical importance in most instances. At the same time, the recomputed regression would indicate when the additional information made available by sales in the latest period changes the estimated values of the index for earlier periods by amounts of sufficient practical importance to warrant revision of previously published estimates. The whole published series might then be revised infrequently if desired. And, if the computational burden of recomputing the regression each period is excessive, it too can be avoided. After obtaining the index for an initial interval of time using the regression method, the index could be estimated for succeeding periods using a variant of the chain method described earlier. Price relatives whose final sales occur in the periods following the initial computation via the regression method could be adjusted to the base period by multiplying them by previously estimated values of the index for their period of initial sale. The geometric mean of these adjusted price relatives could then be taken as the estimate of the index for that period. As our discussion in sections 3 and 5 below suggests, the gain in efficiency of the regression method over the chain method tends to be greatest in the earlier periods of the index. The modification of the chain method described here would seem largely to overcome its greatest weakness, the scarcity of information upon which to base the estimated index for earlier periods.

3. Illustration for the Three-Period Case

To see how the regression method works and to compare it with the method for chaining together price relatives discussed in the introduction, consider estimation of a price index for three periods. Under the assumptions made in $(1), \bar{r}_{01}$, the mean of the price relatives for all pairs with initial transaction in period 0 and final transaction in period 1, is an unbiased estimator of b_1. Another unbiased estimator, which is uncorrelated with $\bar{r}_{01}$, is $(\bar{r}_{02}-\bar{r}_{12})$. Further, given our assumptions about u:

$$\mathrm{var}(\bar{r}_{01}) = \frac{\sigma^2}{n_{01}} \quad \text{and} \quad \mathrm{var}(\bar{r}_{02} - \bar{r}_{12}) = \left(\frac{1}{n_{02}} + \frac{1}{n_{12}}\right)\sigma^2.$$

As is well known, the weighted average of two or more uncorrelated estimators with minimum variance is that in which the separate estimators are weighted in inverse proportion to their variances. Thus, the minimum variance weighted average of $\bar{r}_{01}$ and $(\bar{r}_{02} - \bar{r}_{12})$ is

$$\frac{n_{01}\bar{r}_{01} + \left(\dfrac{n_{02}n_{12}}{n_{02} + n_{12}}\right)(\bar{r}_{02} - \bar{r}_{12})}{n_{01} + \left(\dfrac{n_{02}n_{12}}{n_{02} + n_{12}}\right)} = \frac{n_{01}(n_{02} + n_{12})\bar{r}_{01} + n_{02}n_{12}(\bar{r}_{02} - \bar{r}_{12})}{n_{01}(n_{02} + n_{12}) + n_{02}n_{12}}.$$

Now, consider (3), in the three-period case

$$(x'x) = \left\{ \begin{matrix} (n_{01} + n_{12}) & -n_{12} \\ -n_{12} & (n_{02} + n_{12}) \end{matrix} \right\}$$

$$(x'x)^{-1} = [n_{01}(n_{02} + n_{12}) + n_{02}n_{12}]^{-1} \left\{ \begin{matrix} (n_{02} + n_{12}) & n_{12} \\ n_{12} & (n_{01} + n_{12}) \end{matrix} \right\},$$

$$(x'r) = \left\{ \begin{matrix} n_{01}\bar{r}_{01} - n_{12}\bar{r}_{12} \\ n_{02}\bar{r}_{02} + n_{12}\bar{r}_{12} \end{matrix} \right\}.$$

Substituting in (3) yields

$$\begin{aligned} \hat{b}_1 &= \frac{(n_{02} + n_{12})(n_{01}\bar{r}_{01} - n_{12}\bar{r}_{12}) + n_{12}(n_{02}\bar{r}_{02} + n_{12}\bar{r}_{12})}{n_{01}(n_{02} + n_{12}) + n_{02}n_{12}} \\ &= \frac{n_{01}(n_{02} + n_{12})\bar{r}_{01} + n_{02}n_{12}(\bar{r}_{02} - \bar{r}_{12})}{n_{01}(n_{02} + n_{12}) + n_{02}n_{12}}, \end{aligned} \qquad (6a)$$

which is identical with minimum variance weighted average of $\bar{r}_{01}$ and $(\bar{r}_{02} - \bar{r}_{12})$. Similarly for the second period

$$\hat{b}_2 = \frac{n_{02}(n_{01} + n_{12})\bar{r}_{02} + n_{01}n_{12}(\bar{r}_{01} + \bar{r}_{12})}{n_{01}(n_{02} + n_{12}) + n_{02}n_{12}}. \qquad (6b)$$

In (6b) $\bar{r}_{02}$ and $(\bar{r}_{01} + \bar{r}_{12})$ are, on our assumptions, uncorrelated unbiased estimators of b_2.

We now turn to the chain index discussed in the introduction; the estimators of the logs of the unknown indexes described there are

$$\bar{b}_1 = \bar{r}_{01} \tag{7a}$$

$$\bar{b}_2 = \frac{n_{02}\bar{r}_{02} + n_{12}(\bar{r}_{01} + \bar{r}_{12})}{n_{02} + n_{12}}. \tag{7b}$$

Here the estimator $\bar{b}_1$ is seen to ignore completely the information about b_1 provided by the price relatives for which the final transaction took place in period two, namely, $(\bar{r}_{02} - \bar{r}_{12})$. The estimator $\bar{b}_2$ takes into account both $\bar{r}_{02}$ and $(\bar{r}_{01} + \bar{r}_{12})$ but weights them inefficiently—in proportion to the number of final sales in period two rather than in inverse proportion to their variances.

For the three-period case it is relatively easy to compute the variance of $\bar{b}$ and hence its relative efficiency. On the assumptions we have made about u

$$\text{var}(\bar{b}_1) = \frac{\sigma^2}{n_{01}} \quad \text{and} \quad \text{var}(\bar{b}_2) = \left[\frac{n_{01}(n_{02} + n_{12}) + n_{12}^2}{n_{01}(n_{02} + n_{12})^2}\right]\sigma^2.$$

Since $\text{var}(\hat{b}) = \sigma^2(x'x)^{-1}$:

$$\text{var}(\hat{b}_1) = \frac{(n_{02} + n_{12})\sigma^2}{n_{01}(n_{02} + n_{12}) + n_{02}n_{12}},$$

and similarly for $\hat{b}_2$. Thus the relative efficiencies of $\bar{b}_1$ and $\bar{b}_2$ are:

$$\frac{V(\hat{b}_1)}{V(\bar{b}_1)} = \frac{n_{01}(n_{02} + n_{12})}{n_{01}(n_{02} + n_{12}) + n_{02}n_{12}}, \quad \text{and}$$

$$\frac{V(\hat{b}_2)}{V(\bar{b}_2)} = \frac{n_{01}(n_{01} + n_{12})(n_{02} + n_{12})^2}{n_{01}(n_{01} + n_{12})(n_{02} + n_{12})^2 + n_{02}n_{12}^3}. \tag{8}$$

For $n_{01} = n_{12} = m$, $n_{02} = 2m$, not implausible relative magnitudes, the relative efficiency of $\bar{b}_1$ is 0.6 and that of $\bar{b}_2$ is 0.9; however, as n_{01} goes to zero both relative efficiencies go to zero. This example suggests that the advantage of the regression method is greater for the earlier periods of the index and where there are relatively few sales in the earlier periods. Also, as either n_{02} or n_{12} goes to zero the estimators $\bar{b}$ and $\hat{b}$ become the same and the relative efficiency of $\bar{b}$ goes to one. These results suggest a conjecture which we do not attempt to prove for the general case, namely that the advantage of the regression method for a particular period is greatest where the excess of initial over final transactions in all preceding periods is large and where the number of initial transactions in this particular period is large.

4. Multiple Repeat Sales and Correlated Errors

In many cases there may be data on more than two sales of a given property for the time period covered by the index. If so, there is no unique way to reduce these sales to price relatives, and any way of computing price relatives is likely to run into the problem of correlated residuals.

To see why this is so, let the sales price of the ith property in the tth period, P_{it}, be the product of a property effect, A_i, a period effect, B_t, and a residual effect, V_{it} :

$$P_{it} = A_i B_t V_{it}, \quad \text{or}$$
$$p_{it} = a_i + b_t + v_{it} \tag{9}$$

in logs. We assume that the v's have zero mean, constant variance, and are uncorrelated with each other. Here, the v's represent, for example, the effect on the sales price due to the peculiarities of a particular combination of buyer and seller. If, now, data on sales prices exist for periods t, t' and t'', there are three price relatives which could be computed, namely:

$$r_{itt'} = p_{it'} - p_{it} = -b_t + b_{t'} + (v_{it'} - v_{it})$$
$$r_{itt''} = -b_t + b_{t''} + (v_{it''} - v_{it}) \tag{10}$$
$$r_{it't''} = -b_{t'} + b_{t''} + (v_{it''} - v_{it'}).$$

Under our assumptions about the v's,

$$\text{Var}(r_{itt'}) = \text{Var}(r_{itt''}) = \text{Var}(r_{it't''}) = 2\,\text{Var}(v_{it})$$
$$\text{Cov}(r_{itt'}, r_{itt''}) = \text{Cov}(r_{itt''}, r_{it't''}) = \text{Var}(v_{it}) \tag{11}$$
$$\text{Cov}(r_{itt'}, r_{it't''}) = -\text{Var}(v_{it}).$$

One way out of this problem would be to work directly with sales prices and estimate the property effect for each property along with the period effects or index numbers. To do so would not be computationally feasible, however, with existing computer regression routines.

A more feasible alternative would be to use weighted regression methods, since under the assumptions made above the variance-covariance matrix, M, of the residuals is known up to a scalar. As is well known, the minimum variance linear unbiased estimator is:

$$\hat{b} = (x'M^{-1}x)^{-1}(x'M^{-1}r).$$ (12)

Here, M has +1's down the diagonal, and, if $r_{itt'}$ and $r_{it't''}$ are included, $-\frac{1}{2}$ in the row and column for any pair of relatives involving the same sales price in period t', and 0's elsewhere. In practice the computations might be simplified by dividing the price relatives into two groups, the second containing all n_2 price relatives containing a common sales price. The matrices x, M, and r then become:

$$x = \begin{Bmatrix} x_1 \\ x_2 \end{Bmatrix}, \qquad M = \begin{Bmatrix} I & 0 \\ 0 & M^* \end{Bmatrix}, \qquad r = \begin{Bmatrix} r_1 \\ r_2 \end{Bmatrix},$$

so (12) can be simplified to:

$$\hat{b} = (x_1'x_1 + x_2'M^{*-1}x_2)^{-1}(x_1'r_1 + x_2'M^{*-1}r_2).$$ (13)

In (13), $(x_1'x_1)$ and $(x_1'r_1)$ can be evaluated directly as discussed above. Provided that there are few properties with more than two sales prices for the period covered, it should not be difficult to obtain $(x_2'M^{*-1}x_2)$ and $(x_2'M^{*-1}r_2)$ by direct matrix multiplication.

It might be argued, however, that in addition to the v's in (10), the u's in (1) contain another component, w, which represents the deviation of the relative change in value of a particular property between the periods of initial and final sale from the average of all properties covered by the index. Furthermore, if successive w's for a particular property are uncorrelated with each other, then one clearly should include $r_{itt'}$ and $r_{it't''}$ rather than either of the other two pairs in (10) in calculating the index to avoid correlation of residuals. Without knowing the relative variances of the v's and w's, the method of weighted regression discussed above cannot be applied. Using (3), however, would probably be reasonably efficient if there are few properties with two or more sales prices and if the variance of the v's is small relative to the variances of the w's. In any case, the estimator (3) is unbiased if the u's have zero mean, regardless of their intercorrelation. And (3) is no doubt superior to the chain method because it uses more of the information provided by the data.

5. A Numerical Comparison of the Chain and Regression Methods

The following example, taken from a study by Nourse,[3] illustrates the advantages of the regression method over the chain method of real estate price

Table 3-1. Comparison of Real Estate Price Indexes for a Small Area in St. Louis Estimated by the Chain and Regression Methods

Year	Chain Link Method	Regression Method			Number of Initial and Final Sales in Each Year
	Index 1937 = 1.00	Index 1937 = 1.00	Logarithm of Index	Standard Error in Logarithms	
1937	1.00	1.00	0	—	52
1938	.94	.99	− .0048	.0546	35
1939	2.50	.96	− .0188	.0490	60
1940	1.35	1.05	.0206	.0468	65
1941	2.34	1.07	.0312	.0464	71
1942	3.37	1.41	.1498	.0463	77
1943	2.46	1.52	.1803	.0471	59
1944	2.59	1.51	.1793	.0428	103
1945	2.98	1.75	.2423	.0424	109
1946	3.55	2.10	.3232	.0410	128
1947	4.38	2.34	.3687	.0432	105
1948	4.79	2.59	.4137	.0438	90
1949	4.53	2.21	.3438	.0466	67
1950	5.57	2.79	.4458	.0470	64
1951	5.62	2.90	.4624	.0464	70
1952	5.51	2.99	.4757	.0473	64
1953	5.72	2.96	.4718	.0507	50
1954	4.82	2.90	.4620	.0540	39
1955	5.51	3.09	.4901	.0499	47
1956	6.34	3.38	.5288	.0580	31
1957	5.74	3.06	.4863	.0528	44
1958	5.77	3.13	.4955	.0551	38
1959	4.85	2.62	.4184	.0523	44
					1512 Total

index construction. Indeed, it was the erratic behavior of the index estimated by the chain method that first prompted us to devise a better method.

In this study it was desired to construct an index of the prices of real properties for a small area of the near northwest part of St. Louis. The price data were obtained from the amount of tax stamps affixed to warranty deeds.[c]

---

[c]Federal tax stamps must be affixed to the warranty deed in an amount not less than $.55 per $500.00 of value conveyed. While the law does not prohibit affixing more stamps, there would seem to be no incentive to pay a higher tax than necessary. But since tax stamps are available only in multiples of $.55, only a $500.00 range of values can be determined from the tax stamp amount. In this study the sales price was taken to be the upper limit of this $500.00 range, since studies cited by Tonty et al.[6] indicate that the actual amount is generally greater than the mid-point of the range and frequently at the upper limit. These latter studies also suggest that the difference between the actual consideration and that estimated from the tax stamp amount is less than 5 percent.

Chart 1. Comparison of Real Estate Price Indexes for a Small Area in St. Louis estmated by the Chain and Regression Methods

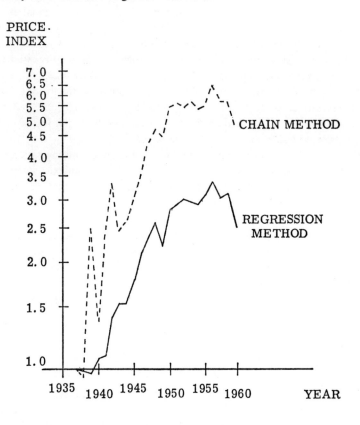

Values estimated from tax stamp values were then adjusted on the basis of other information contained in the warranty deed. For any transaction in which only a partial interest was conveyed, the value indicated by tax stamps was divided by the fraction of the interest conveyed. Where an outstanding mortgage was assumed by the buyer and its amount was stated in the deed, this amount was added to the equity conveyed by the deed; otherwise, this transaction was not included in the study. A transaction was not included if more than one property was conveyed by the deed, unless all of the properties conveyed were in the area studied and had been transferred together at least twice during the period covered by the study.

Next, price relatives and their logs were computed from these adjusted tax stamp values. To obtain the regression estimate, equation (3), of the price index, the number and sum of the logs of price relatives with initial and final sales in a particular pair of years were entered above the diagonals of two 23 by 23 matrices. The elements of $(x'x)$ and $(x'r)$ were then evaluated using the rules described in section 2, above: The tth diagonal element of ($x'x$) was found by adding elements of the tth column of the number of price relatives matrix down to the diagonal and then across the tth row; the t, t'th off diagonal element of ($x'x$) is, of course, the negative of the corresponding element of the number of price relatives matrix. The tth element of the 23-dimensional vector ($x'r$) was found by adding all elements of the sums of logs of price relatives matrix down the tth column to the diagonal and then subtracting those elements across the tth row. The information so obtained was then inserted into a computer regression routine prior to the matrix inversion phase. The remainder of the computations were performed by the computer, and its output included the logs of the estimated index and their standard errors.

Price indexes estimated from these data by the chain and regression methods are shown in Table 3-1 and plotted in Chart 1. The two indexes diverge greatly in the years prior to 1943. In fact, most of the difference in the levels of the two is accounted for by the change in the chain index from 1938 to 1939. In addition, the year-to-year changes in the index estimated by the chain method are very erratic from 1938 to 1943, much more so than the regression estimate of the index. For 1944 and following years, however, the indexes estimated by the two methods are very similar apart from the higher level of the chain estimate. We suspect that the major reason for the difference between the two estimates is the fact that there were relatively few final sales upon which to base the chain estimate for the earlier years.

References

1. Griliches, Z., "Hedonic price indexes for automobiles: An econometric analysis of quality change," U.S. Congress, Joint Economic Committee, GOVERNMENT PRICE STATISTICS. Hearings, January 24, 1961. Washington: Government Printing Office, 1961. Pp. 173-96.

2. Laurenti, Luigi, PROPERTY VALUES AND RACE. Berkeley: University of California Press, 1960.

3. Nourse, Hugh O., "The Effect of Public Housing on Property Values in St. Louis." Unpublished Ph.D. dissertation, Department of Economics, University of Chicago, 1962.

4. Pendleton, William C., "The Value of Accessibility." Unpublished Ph.D. dissertation, Department of Economics, University of Chicago, 1963.

5. Suits, Daniel B., "Use of dummy variables in regression equations," JOURNAL OF THE AMERICAN STATISTICAL ASSOCIATION, 52 (1957), 548-51.

6. Tonty, Robert L., et al., "Reliability of deed samples as indicators of land market activity," LAND ECONOMICS, XXX (1954), 47-8.

7. Wenzlick, Roy, "As I see the fluctuations in the selling prices of

single-family residences," THE REAL ESTATE ANALYST, XXI (December 24, 1952), 541-8.

8. Wyngarden, Herman, AN INDEX OF LOCAL REAL ESTATE PRICES. Michigan Business Studies, Vol. 1, No. 2. Ann Arbor: University of Michigan, 1927.

4

Redistribution of Income
from Public Housing

The development of cost-benefit analysis to evaluate public investments has caused neglect of the income distribution effects of these investments. Cost-benefit analysis attempts to evaluate the return on a given public investment relative to other possible investments. The important information is whether or not the investment causes a net increase in production, and if so, how much. Some public investments such as Public Housing and Urban Renewal specifically attempt to redistribute income and wealth from one sector of the population to another. Even those public investments undertaken primarily to increase produc tion are opposed or supported because of their redistribution effects on special interest groups. Modern economic welfare theory states that the economist is in no position to evaluate which is the better of two states of affairs that differ by taking income from one group and redistributing it to others. Nevertheless, redistribution of income does take place, it does influence interest groups, and it is often the purpose of certain public investments. It is, therefore, worthwhile to investigate.

This study describes a simple model for tracing the impact of public housing on income distribution. The assumptions in the model refer to average conditions in the United States. Modifications in the assumption would be necessary to determine the impact of public housing on the distribution of income in a particular community. Perhaps the general approach can be applied to other public services to determine their impact on income distribution.

Function of Public Housing in the
Government Budget

We can divide the economic functions of the government budget into three categories. The first function is the reallocation of resources to more efficient uses. To the non-economist this would appear to be very narrow, but it in fact encompasses such activities as the courts, national defense, control of monopoly, and public utilities. The second function is the redistribution of income and wealth toward a "norm" decided by the majority. The graduated income tax and public welfare payments are examples. The third function is the stabilization of employment.[2]

Many government programs, which are in reality redistributions of income,

Source: Reprinted from NATIONAL TAX JOURNAL, vol. 19, no. 11 (March 1966).

are not openly acknowledged as such. The main example is the farm price support program. Income is redistributed to farmers via control of farm product prices. In the process, reallocation of farm products and input takes place because prices cause individuals and businesses to use more or less of the commodity. Public housing falls in the same category. Housing is a service that can be, and is, provided by the economy without government support. One person has argued that public housing is the responsibility of government because it is considered so meritorious by the population that the government should provide certain minimum standards.[3] But the reason that people cannot provide minimum standard housing for themselves is that their incomes are too low. Housing is visible, and food consumption is not. Thus, others can see how bad housing is, but cannot see the diet of the poor. The remedy may really be a direct redistribution of income, but the public housing program is aimed at correcting only one symptom of poverty—substandard housing. Public housing is a redistribution of income in kind. The taxed provide better housing to the poor who cannot afford it.

The Public Housing Operation[4]

A local housing authority, with the advice and consent of the local government, decides on a plan and a location for the public housing development. Nevertheless, to receive Federal assistance the plan must also be approved by the Public Housing Administration (PHA). In the development stage, PHA may make short-term or long-term loans to the local authority to aid in the development, acquisition, or administration of low-rent housing. Funds for lending are raised by outstanding obligations for purchase by the Secretary of the Treasury. The total of all these obligations supporting all loans was at one time (1959) limited to $1.5 billion. The interest rate charged was that on Federal bonds with terms up to 40 years.

Once the housing is constructed, all of the development and construction costs are transferred into a long-term debt financed by public housing bonds sold by the local housing authority. The income from these bonds is tax-free, so that the interest rate is low. Buyers are willing to receive a lower income since it will not be taxed.

In order to make decent housing available to tenants with low incomes, rents in the public housing projects are set at 20 percent of their adjusted gross income. Such rents, however, will not pay for the cost of constructing and operating the public housing projects. Since local governments cannot make up the difference between the receipts and costs of public housing, local housing authorities could not continue to provide low-rent housing unless subsidized. The difference between receipts and costs of operation (including interest, amortization of bonds, and operation and maintenance) is subsidized by the PHA through an annual contribution.

Annual contributions may not be paid for more than 40 years from the first payment and can be no greater than the Federal rate of interest plus 2 percent of project development or acquisition cost. In practice the annual contribution is no greater than the level debt service (interest payments and amortization of the debt) on local authority bonds. If operating income is greater than the other expenditures for a local authority, annual contributions are reduced by this "residual receipt." PHA has paid 62 percent of the maximum that it could have paid from 1947-1957.

After the 40 year period the local agency normally owns the project free and clear, except that any "residual receipts" must be paid to PHA (if all annual contributions have not been paid back) and to local public bodies that have contributed through tax exemption in proportion to their several contributions.

In private real estate operations there is an expenditure for property taxes. Since public housing is a government operation it is tax exempt. To avoid the political animosity of local governments PHA has the projects pay 10 percent of their receipts from tenants as a payment in lieu of taxes.

The public housing operation can be summarized in Figure 4-1, which illustrates the main flows of receipts and expenditures.

Since there are no effective limitations on the capital cost of public housing projects, Congress has set room construction cost limitations. The rule, however, does not cover site acquisition and improvement, non-dwelling construction and equipment and other costs. Thus, there is no control over land costs except through design rules about the amount of land per room. To maximize the number of rooms for any given congressional appropriation, it is in the interest of PHA to allow as little land as possible per dwelling in order to spread the money over more units. Nevertheless, PHA has set total per unit construction cost ceilings. PHA approval requires local authorities to come under these standards. For example, PHA Commissioner Slusser has said, "This ceiling ($17,000 on total development cost per dwelling unit in high-cost areas) is also an effort on our part to produce the maximum number of low-rent housing units under the total authorization for annual contributions."[5]

Shift of Flow of Funds from before Public Housing to after Public Housing—A Simple Model

The constantly changing incidents and forces in a real economy blur the impact of any single action. Therefore, a number of simplifying assumptions will be made in order to analyze the impact of public housing on income distribution. After a conclusion is drawn from this simple world, some of the assumptions will be relaxed in order to see how the conclusions might be changed in a more complicated situation.

The following simplifying assumptions are made:

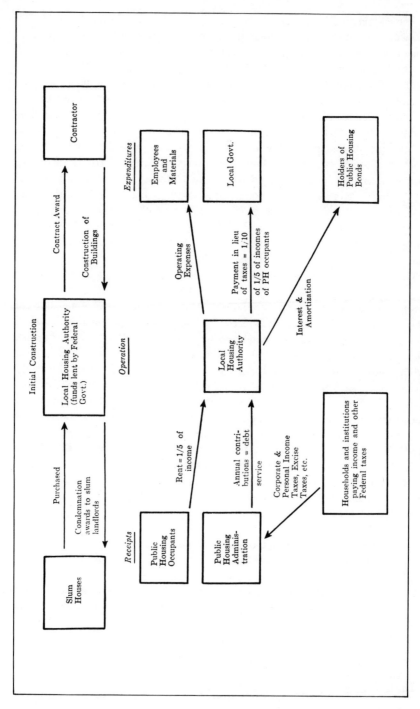

Figure 4-1. Public Housing Transactions

1. The public housing project replaces slum housing. The same area is encompassed and the same number of housing units are available before and after public housing, although the public housing units may be high-rise with more open space.
2. There is no relocation. Initially we shall not worry with the problem of how to do it, but we shall assume residents move from slum housing to public housing on the same site.
3. The occupants pay 20 percent of their income on rents excluding utilities to the slum landlord before public housing and the same amount to the local housing authority after public housing. Actually, this may not be a bad assumption. In 1960 the census shows that the median gross rent to income ratio for tenants in substandard housing inside metropolitan areas was 21 percent.[a] Public Housing Authority data show that the median gross rent to gross income ratio for public housing tenants was 20 percent.[b] The percent distribution, however, was not the same. Twenty-seven percent of tenants in private substandard housing paid 35 percent or more of their income on gross rent. Only 7 percent of public housing occupants paid 36 percent or more of their income on gross rent.
4. Slum housing is owned by persons other than the occupants. In 1960 77 percent of substandard housing inside metropolitan areas were tenant occupied.[6]
5. The distribution of incomes of slum landlords is the same as the general population excluding those occupying the slum housing turned into public housing.
6. The local housing authority pays to the local government sums in lieu of taxes equal to 10 percent of its rent income from tenants.
7. Public housing is financed by the sale of bonds issued by the local housing

[a]Calculated from Table B-4 in U.S. Bureau of the Census, U.S. CENSUS OF HOUSING 1960, vol. II, part I. The distribution was as follows:

Gross Rent as % of Income	Per Cent of Tenants in Substandard Housing Inside Metropolitan Areas
Under 10	12
10 through 14	16
15 through 19	13
20 through 24	10
25 through 34	12
35 and over	27
Not Computed	10

authority. The slum landlords will purchase local public housing bonds with the condemnation awards they receive. It will be shown, however, that others will also have to purchase the bonds. The annual debt service of interest payments and amortization paid to the individuals is subsidized through the annual contribution of the Federal Government to the local housing authority.

8. Occupants of public housing have incomes so low that they pay no income taxes to the Federal Government. The following table shows the actual percentage distribution of net family income in 1959.

The net income in Table 4-1 is net of deductions allowable by the Public Housing Authority before rent is determined. It is the income determining the families' rent. In 1959, total family income was 3 percent higher on the average. The personal income tax for a married person with two dependents was zero in 1959, if gross income was less than $2,675. Sixty percent of public housing tenants had incomes less than $2,500. Furthermore, 97 percent of public housing tenants had incomes less than $5,000. A married family with two children would have been taxed only $416 in 1959, if their income had been $4,950 to $5,000. In 1964 the tax would

bCalculated from data sent to author by Louis S. Katz, Director, Statistics Branch, the Public Housing Authority, dated July 27, 1965. The distribution was as follows:

Gross Rent of Families in Low-Rent Public
Housing as a Per Cent of Anticipated
Annual Total Family Income (Gross)
1960

Per Cent	Per Cent of Families
Under 14.00	2.6
14.00–15.99	5.0
16.00–17.99	20.5
18.00–19.99	23.6
20.00–21.99	20.0
22.00–23.99	6.2
24.00–25.99	3.5
26.00–27.99	2.7
28.00–29.99	2.5
30.00–31.99	2.3
32.00–33.99	2.0
34.00–35.99	1.7
36.00–37.99	1.4
38.00–39.99	1.1
40.00 and over	4.9

Table 4-1
Incomes of Families in Low-Rent Public Housing, 1959

Net Family Income	Per Cent of Families
Less than $1,000	8.0
$1,000–1,499	14.9
1,500–1,999	17.5
2,000–2,499	16.5
2,500–2,999	13.7
3,000–3,499	10.4
3,500–3,999	7.7
4,000–4,499	5.5
4,500–4,999	3.0
5,000–5,999	2.0
6,000 and over	0.9

Source: Public Housing Authority, letter to the author from Louis S. Katz, Director, Statistics Branch, July 27, 1965.

have only been $321. (A family of eight earning $5,000 would be exempt from income taxes.) These figures are only an indication of the actual tax. Each individual case would have to be calculated before summing to get the total income tax payments by the tenants.

The table below shows the receipts and expenditures of the slum landlord before public housing. Now assume that the local housing authority buys the

Landlord

Receipts	Expenditures
20 per cent of income of tenants	Federal income taxes Operating expenses Property taxes

slums from the landlords and pays the market value, that is, the present worth of the expected annual net receipts. The authority demolishes all of the houses and rebuilds public housing by contracting with a private builder. Since the costs to the local authority are greater than the value of the old housing, more funds are needed. Other purchasers of the bonds, in addition to the slum landlords, will have to be found to finance the project.

After the project is constructed the receipts and expenditures of the local authority will be as shown in the table below.

Local Housing Authority

Receipts	Expenditures
20 per cent of income of tenants	Payments in lieu of taxes equal to 10% of 20% of tenant income
Annual contributions from Federal Govt. to service debt	Operating expenses
	Interest and amortization payments to public housing bondholders

The economic impact of the project begins with its construction. If the construction workers would otherwise have been unemployed, the construction of the project causes an increase in total national income. If the workers would otherwise have been building other buildings, offices, apartments, houses, etc., there would be no change in total national income, but the kind of buildings constructed would change. If the necessary workers in construction are too few as a result of this increase in demand, as is likely to be the case if there is full employment, the increased need for construction workers draws workers from other employments. While the total national income would increase somewhat, income would shift in favor of construction workers and their employers. The total value of public housing, however, has been small. Public housing construction has represented less than 2 percent of total value of new construction put in place annually from 1947 through 1963.

Local government receipts will change depending upon the way that payments in lieu of taxes relate to the previous property taxes. In fact, there is a relation between the two. Property taxes are some proportion of property values, say some ratio K. The property value is the present worth of expected net incomes from the property. These relationships are shown in the following equations.

$$P_0 = \frac{S_1}{(1+i)} + \frac{S_2}{(1+i)^2} + \cdots + \frac{S_n}{(1+i)^n}$$

where S = annual net income
i = market rate of interest (rate of return on alternative investments with equal risks)
n = life of investment or time necessary to recapture principal
P_0 = property value

We shall consider the net annual income to be constant over the life of the investment in the slum property. It is equal to 20 percent of tenant income less operating expenses and taxes. In this case, property value can be calculated by the following formula.

$$P_0 = S \left[\frac{(1 + i)^n - 1}{i(1 + i)^n} \right]$$

or,

$$P_0 = .20y - E(.20y) \left[\frac{(1+i)^n - 1}{i(1+i)^n} \right] = .20y(1 - E) \left[\frac{(1+i)^n - 1}{i(1+i)^n} \right].$$

where E = ratio of operating expenses and taxes to total receipts
y = total income of tenants
$.20y$ = rent payments of tenants

The property taxes are as follows:

$$T = K P_0$$

$$T = K(1 - E) \left[\frac{(1 + i)^n - 1}{i(1 + i)^n} \right] .20y$$

where T = property tax
K = proportion of present worth of property

The payments in lieu of taxes are as follows:

$$L = .10 (.20y)$$

where L = payment in lieu of taxes.

Thus, payments in lieu of taxes will equal property taxes paid by slum landlords when the following equality is true:

$$.10(.20y) = K(1 - E) \left[\begin{array}{c} L = T \\ \frac{(1 + i)^n - 1}{i(1 + i)^n} \end{array} \right] .20y$$

or when

$$.10 = K(1 - E) \left[\frac{(1 + i)^n - 1}{i(1 + i)^n} \right]$$

By making reasonable assumptions for the variables on the right side of the equation we can see whether that term is greater or less than 10 percent. If it is greater than 10 percent, property taxes paid by slum landlords would be greater than payments in lieu of taxes. If the right hand term is less than 10 percent, the payments in lieu of taxes made by the local housing authority would be greater than the property taxes paid by the former slum landlords.

K ranged between 0.0076 and 0.0384 with a median of 0.0148 in a survey made in 1956.[c] According to one informed source, a reasonable assumption to make for values for E, i, and n are as follows, providing we assume that the owners maintain minimum standards and do not expect any resale value at the end of n years:[7]

$$E = .75 - .85, \quad i = 15 - 20\%, \quad n = 15$$

Using these values the right term above ranges from 0.01 to 0.05 and is less than 0.10. Thus, the payments in lieu of taxes are greater than the property taxes formerly paid by the slum landlords.

A 1952 study of the Public Housing Administration indicated that payments in lieu of taxes for 412 permanently financed completed low-rent projects in 34 states and the District of Columbia were greater than the last annual property tax levy on sites prior to acquisition for low-rent use. Total payments in lieu of taxes were \$3,398,000, while the previous tax levy was \$1,576,000. In addition, total outstanding tax delinquencies amounted to \$3,403,000, which the local authorities paid. Some people argue that the local government actually loses taxes because the public housing projects would bring in many more dollars through property taxes, if they were assessed on the basis of replacement cost. For example, in the above survey, property taxes on the public housing projects, if privately owned, would have amounted to \$12,448,000. But this is an unreasonable comparison. Privately owned housing for these low-income people would never bring in that much revenue. The tax on the previous slum housing is a better indicator of the alternative tax receipts.[8]

We shall assume that real estate operating employment shifts from the private market to the public housing operation so that no redistribution of income takes place in this market. Wages will be equal before and after, if local housing authorities pay the going rates.

The most important shift is the shift from the taxed to the occupants of public housing. The recipients of the income redistribution are the occupants of the public housing who are paying less than the housing units are worth. There has been an increase in taxes by the Federal Government to cover the annual contribution and the administrative costs of the PHA. Since the income tax is a graduated tax, increases in taxes come more from upper income groups than lower income groups. The former slum landlords and other holders of public housing bonds are exempt from taxes, but the return on the bonds is lower than

---

[c]Survey of 85 metropolitan areas made in 1956 by Roy Wenzlick Research Corporation, St. Louis, Missouri.

the taxed return on alternative investments of equal risk. If interest rates are determined competitively, they are getting no more than they would from the alternative investments. The funds for the subsidy come from households and corporations not holding public housing bonds, not living in public housing, and who pay Federal taxes. Nevertheless, public housing bondholders share in the burden of the tax because their income is less than it would have been if there had been no increase in taxes to subsidize public housing.[d] For the rate of return on tax exempt bonds to continue to be equal to the net rate on alternative investments after taxes, the rate on tax exempts will have to fall to compensate for the increased taxes on alternative investments.

The total shift in funds through Federal taxes must include the amount of the annual contributions and administrative costs of the Public Housing Administration necessary to subsidize low-rent housing projects. These expenditures for the public housing program since 1950 are shown in Table 4-2. Column four shows the total subsidy.

More Realistic Assumptions

The first assumption to relax is that the slum dwellers move from their slum housing directly into public housing on the same site. It takes time to construct

Table 4-2

Administrative Expenditures and Annual Contributions Paid of the Public Housing Program in the United States

Fiscal Year Ending June 30	Administrative Expenditures (in millions)	Annual Contributions (in millions)	Total Subsidy (in millions)	Units Eligible	Total Subsidy per Unit
1950	$ 6.3	$ 5.7	$ 12.0	146,549	$ 82
1951	9.7	9.1	18.8	145,703	129
1952	9.3	12.6	21.9	156,084	140
1953	8.2	25.9	34.1	204,815	166
1954	6.6	44.5	51.1	259,116	197
1955	7.4	66.6	74.0	304,383	243
1956	9.1	81.7	90.8	343,907	264
1957	10.0	90.6	100.6	365,896	275
1958	11.6	98.8	110.4	374,172	295
1959	12.4	115.4	127.8	401,467	318
1960	12.4	131.2	143.6	425,850	337
1961	13.9	145.3	189.2	467,936	362
1962	13.9	159.3	173.2	482,714	359
1963	15.0	176.4	191.4	511,047	374
1964 and 1965 not available					

Source: U.S. Housing and Home Finance Agency, *Annual Reports.*

[d]People who buy tax exempt bonds gain by reduction of their income tax burden, if the marginal tax rate on their income is greater than the difference in interest rates between investments of equal risk but one of which is tax exempt. We have assumed, however, that the public housing bondholders, except for slum landlords, have shifted from other tax exempt investments. If there is an increase in the total funds in tax exempt bonds because of the public housing offerings, the interest rate on tax exempts would have to increase to increase the willingness of people to buy, and there would be a reduction in the tax burden of these bondholders.

a project. The residents in the slum housing move elsewhere. After the project is completed, residents are selected from all eligible slum dwellers in the city. The construction of the public housing units temporarily reduces the available housing and probably induces some crowding. Once built, reduction in crowding will depend upon the number of public housing units made available.

If the same number of units is made available in public housing as were on the site prior to its construction, the previous analysis stands. But suppose that more units or fewer units are constructed in public housing. In St. Louis, for example, some projects reduced the number of units on the site: Clinton Peabody Terrace, George L. Vaughn, and Darst Apartments. Others increased the number of housing units on the site: Carr Square Village, John J. Cochran Garden Apartments, and the Pruitt-Igoe complex.

If the number of housing units on the site is reduced, the direct impact on income distribution is changed in the following ways. The subsidy through annual contributions is less, so that income redistribution of housing in kind is less. Payments in lieu of taxes are less, so that they may be less than property taxes on the previous slum property. Some neighborhood stores may lose business to stores in other parts of the city where increased crowding takes place to compensate for the reduction of housing space.

If the number of housing units on the public housing site is increased, the direct change in income distribution through annual contributions is increased. There is a greater shift from taxpayers to the public housing occupants. Furthermore, there is a shift in favor of local government. More receipts will be received through payments in lieu of taxes than were received through property taxes. Greater density may increase local government expenditures, although fire hazards are down, and what evidence there is suggests that police calls decrease.[9] Occupancy in other slum areas has been reduced making it possible to clear these old slums for urban renewal, highways, etc. If they are not condemned and purchased at market value, the owners experience a loss of income directly attributable to the construction of public housing. Another indirect effect may be on stores near the project. The adjacent stores may experience increased sales at the expense of the more distant stores.

Another assumption was that the public housing occupants did not pay any income taxes. It probably is not a bad assumption, but if it is false, the redistribution of income from the taxed to the public housing occupants is less.

Another difficulty is our assumption that the slum properties are assessed at market value. This is not true. Nevertheless, if all property is assessed at 30 percent of market value (or some other constant percentage), slum property would pay its fair share of property taxes with respect to market value. If property is assessed on the basis of the replacement cost of the structure rather than on the basis of income earned from the property, slum properties may not pay their fair share of taxes. The value of slum properties over fifty years old estimated on the basis of replacement cost would be less than the value estimated on the basis of net income. Therefore, slum properties may be undertaxed. If they are undertaxed, local government revenues after public housing would be higher than estimated with our previous assumptions.

But this creates a difficulty in evaluating the impact of public housing on the former slum landlord. Does the local housing authority pay a sum equal to the present worth of the expected net annual incomes, or does the authority pay the slum landlord a sum equal to only the replacement cost of the property? The rule in most jurisdictions is that the value of condemned property be based on what it would bring in the market, so that slum property would be condemned at market value.[10]

Two other points need to be brought up. One is that the slum landlords may receive more than the market value of their property. Since the court decision is based on market value, there is no indication that this is systematically the case unless there should be fraud. The other is that the construction companies may profit excessively from the construction of public housing. As long as there is open bidding for these contracts, there is no reason to suspect excessive profit.

Conclusion

Now we may summarize the various shifts in income that result from the development and operation of public housing.

The slum landlord has lost income as a result of public housing, and his business has been taken over by the government. Slum landlords and other public housing bondholders find their net income reduced because the increased tax to pay for the subsidy forces the interest rate on tax exempt bonds to fall. Some employment in real estate has shifted from the private sector to the public sector.

The low-income families have gained. Although their average rent expenditures remain the same, they now occupy new standard housing. Some may contribute to their own rent through their income tax payments.

The taxpayer has lost. His income has been reduced by the amount of the annual contributions and administrative costs of the Public Housing Administration necessary to subsidize low-rent housing projects. In 1963 0.2 percent of all Federal expenditures went to subsidize 511,047 units.

Construction workers gain with the shift of resources of the economy into the construction of public housing. This shift has been small. Public housing construction has represented less than 2 percent of total value of new construction put in place annually from 1947-1963.

Local governments have gained through the increased receipts from payments in lieu of taxes above the previous payments of property taxes. They gain more if public housing increases the density of an area, since this would increase the payments in lieu of taxes over previous property taxes. They also gain more if the previous slum properties were undertaxed.

The Public Housing Authority has an incentive to obtain the most units per dollar in order to spread the funds it obtains from Congress to as many congressional districts as possible. This causes them to establish rules to restrict the cost per dwelling unit, and to lower land costs by establishing minimum ratios of land per room. These rules are also needed because there is nothing in the structure of the legislation to cause the local housing authorities to find ways of minimizing costs. The only other restriction on the expenditures of local authorities is that their operating expenses be equal to or less than receipts from tenants.

The analysis of the impact of public housing on income distribution has revealed those groups that tend to gain or lose as a result of the construction of housing projects. It has not implied excess profits for any particular group, but has indicated those interest groups whose relative income shares of the total national income will tend to change as a result of public housing.

Notes

1. This paper is based in part on research supported by a grant from the National Institute of Mental Health, Grant No. MH-09189. Alvin Gouldner and Lee Rainwater have provided encouragement. Walter McMahon made many comments on an early draft that has been incorporated in the paper. The author is responsible for the results.

2. Richard A. Musgrave, THE THEORY OF PUBLIC FINANCE (New York: McGraw-Hill Book Company, Inc., 1959), Chapter 1.

3. Ibid.

4. The material for this section is drawn mainly from Robert M. Fisher, TWENTY YEARS OF PUBLIC HOUSING (New York: Harper and Brothers, Publishers, 1959).

5. Ibid., p. 151.

6. Calculated from U.S. Bureau of the Census, U.S. CENSUS OF HOUSING, 1960, vol. II, part I.

7. Conversation with Mr. Anthony Ciareglio, Member of the American Institute of Real Estate Appraisers, and President of Roy Wenzlick & Company, St. Louis, Missouri.

8. Fisher, op. cit., pp. 183-206. Fisher does not evaluate the alternative ways of estimating the property taxes that would have accrued to the local government, if there were no public housing. The analysis above is my own evaluation.

9. Study by St. Louis Police Department, unpublished.

10. American Institute of Real Estate Appraisers, THE APPRAISAL OF REAL ESTATE, 1964, p. 54.

5

Redistribution of Income from the Pruitt-Igoe Public Housing Projects

Chapter 4 dealt with a simple model for tracing the impact of public housing on income distribution. The assumptions in the model referred to average conditions in the United States. In this chapter the original assumptions will be modified to fit the Pruitt-Igoe housing projects in St. Louis, and will attempt to estimate the redistribution of income resulting from the construction and occupancy of the Pruitt-Igoe apartments in St. Louis.

Critical Assumptions for Pruitt-Igoe Projects in Analysis of the Shift of Flow of Funds

The first of the simplifying assumptions made in the previous chapter was that public housing replaced substandard housing with an identical number of units. In the case of the Pruitt-Igoe project this is not a good assumption. In this housing area 2,750 public housing units replaced 705 substandard units.[1] Before construction of public housing there were 10.1 and 11.2 dwelling units per acre in the area. After public housing there were 54.6 and 44.4 dwelling units per acre. Thus, in this particular project slum housing was replaced by many more units than were demolished.

The second assumption was that no relocation from outside the area took place. Since the density of units per acre increased, families were relocated not only from within the area, but from all over the black-occupied areas of the city, which for the most part were also slum areas.[2]

A third assumption was that families paid 20 percent of their income on rents to the slum landlord before public housing and the same amount to the local housing authority after entering public housing. Data presented for United States metropolitan areas indicated that this was a good assumption. Data on the Pruitt-Igoe projects have been obtained from the St. Louis Housing Authority. Rent and income data were obtained for families moving into the Pruitt-Igoe housing units between July 1964 and July 1965.[3] Although not representative of all the occupants in the Pruitt-Igoe housing projects, the data do, nevertheless, yield information on the rent-income ratio for families moving into the projects.

The rents for public housing units were listed as gross rents. Gross rents included about $15 for utilities—water, gas, electricity, fuel—and a range and a refrigerator. The monthly rent before public housing is listed without indication as to whether it was gross rent, net rent, or a mixture of the two. Without specific information, it is best to assume that the data on previous monthly rents most likely represents a mixture of gross and net rent, that is, sometimes including utilities and sometimes not. Thus, for a before-to-after comparison the data are not exactly perfect. The distribution of the rent-income ratio before and after entering public housing is shown in Table 5-1. The median rent-income ratio before entering public housing was 23 percent. The median rent-income ratio after entering public housing was 24 percent. Thus, these ratios are about equal as assumed, but are probably higher than the assumed 20 percent.

The fourth assumption was that the previous slum housing was owned by persons other than the occupants. In 1950 before construction of Pruitt-Igoe apartments 91 percent of the previous housing units in the area were tenant-occupied.[4] There is no way to check the fifth assumption, that the distribution of incomes of slum landlords is the same as that of the general population excluding those occupying the slum housing demolished for public housing.

The sixth assumption was that the model local housing authority pays to the local government sums in lieu of taxes equal to 10 percent of its net rental income from tenants. The St. Louis Housing Authority does agree to pay 10 percent of its net rental income as a payment in lieu of taxes. In 1964 it made payments in lieu of taxes of $61,800 for the Pruitt project and $40,470 for the Igoe project.[5] This would indicate a net rental income of $1,033,700 for the year from the two projects. The Housing Authority states that the annual rental income is approximately $1,315,000. Since utilities would only amount to

Table 5-1
Rent-Income Ratio, Families Entering Pruitt-Igoe Housing Project, July 1964-July 1965

Rent-Income Ratio	Distribution of Ratio Before Entering Public Housing		Distribution of Gross Ratio After Entering Public Housing	
	Number of Families	Percent	Number of Families	Percent
Less than 10%	3	1.8	0	0
10-14%	19	11.4	3	1.3
15-19%	38	22.8	50	21.3
20-24%	30	18.0	67	28.5
25-34%	34	20.4	46	19.6
35% and over	42	25.3	69	29.4
Not computed[a]	69			
Total families	235	100	235	100

Source: Calculated from St. Louis Housing Authority, REPORT ON FAMILIES MOVING INTO LOW-RENT HOUSING.

[a]Not computed are families whose previous rent was unknown or was zero. The latter were excluded because part of the family income may have been housing. To calculate the rent-income ratio would require imputing a rent, adding it as part of income, and calculating the ratio. The data for doing this were unavailable.

$41,250, the increased net rental income of $1,273,750 would be received, if the units were fully occupied. The difference of about $240,000 reflects in part the high vacancy rate on these units. If the projects were fully occupied the net rental income would generate $24,000 additional revenue per year to the city over the $102,270 paid now. In addition to these payments the Housing Authority pays directly for street lighting, street maintenance, and garbage collection. Private apartments and houses in the city receive these services free.

The seventh of the simplifying assumptions was that the previous slum landlords plus additional investors bought the public housing bonds financing the housing project, and that the federal government subsidized the public housing operation by paying all the interest and amortization payments of the outstanding debt. Recent studies indicate that the slum landlords shifted their ownership of property from the older slums to newer areas.[6] Thus, investors purchased all of the public housing bonds. The St. Louis Housing Authority indicates that the actual annual federal contribution to the Pruitt-Igoe projects is $1,420,500. In addition to the annual contribution the subsidy includes the project's share of the administrative costs of the Public Housing Administration. In 1963 the PHA administrative costs per unit were about $29.[7] Thus, the total federal subsidy for the Pruitt-Igoe apartments would be $1,500,250 on the basis of the 2,750 units in the two projects.

The eighth and final assumption was that the public housing tenants have incomes so low that they pay no income taxes to the federal government. On the basis of information on income, family size, family characteristics, and public assistance, the income taxes paid by tenants moving into the Pruitt-Igoe project from July 1964 to July 1965 were calculated. The distribution of estimated income taxes paid in 1965 is shown in Table 5-2. Of the 235 families for which there were data, at least 186 would have paid no federal income tax. Furthermore, taxes were probably overestimated because in many cases additional deductions that could have been made for child care were not taken into

Table 5-2
Estimated 1965 Federal Income Taxes, Families Entering Pruitt-Igoe Housing Project, July 1964-July 1965

Estimate of Income Tax	Number of Families
0	186
$ 1- 50	13
51-100	11
101-250	21
251-500	4
	235

Source: Calculated from St. Louis Housing Authority, REPORT ON FAMILIES MOVING INTO LOW-RENT HOUSING.

account. Nevertheless, the mean estimated tax paid per family was $26. Of this amount $0.05 would have been allocated to the public housing subsidy by the federal government. This is a miniscule percent of the $545 subsidy per unit, so that our assumption continues to be a good one.

Shift of Flow of Funds from before Public Housing to after Public Housing

The economic impact of the project begins with its construction. The kind of impact depends upon whether the economy is fully employed. The Pruitt-Igoe projects were completed in several stages. The completion dates were September 1955, April 1956, and May 1956. The bulk of the construction activity would have been in 1955, which was a booming year for construction in the nation as well as in St. Louis. In 1955 construction employment in St. Louis reached a peak of 45,800, an increase of 5 percent over 1954. In 1956 construction employment in St. Louis fell 3 percent.[8] Unemployment was nominal during this period. Unemployment was 5.6 percent of the national civilian labor force in 1954, but decreased to 4.4 percent in 1955.[9] Thus, construction of the housing projects took place during a period of full employment. During such a period the increased need for construction workers would cause a shift in employment from other occupations and from other areas to the St. Louis area. This shift may not have been very large, since the construction contracts of $31,738,706 on the projects represented only 5 percent of gross capital formation in St. Louis in 1955.[10] To the extent construction took place in 1954 it alleviated unemployment and had a multiplier effect on total income received in the city.

After construction rental receipts from tenants flow to the model housing authority instead of to private property owners. Instead of property tax receipts from the slum landlords, the city receives payments in lieu of taxes from the housing authority. In addition, specifically, there is the shift of funds from the federal government to the fiscal agent of the housing authority to pay the debt service on the bonds.

The local government receipts will change depending upon the way that payments in lieu of taxes relate to the previous property taxes. With the simplifying assumptions in Chapter 4 the payments in lieu of taxes amounted to at least twice as much as the previous property tax receipts. In the case of the Pruitt-Igoe projects the payments in lieu of taxes may be greater than the previous tax receipts by an even greater percentage for two reasons. First, the number of dwelling units has increased. Second, the projects make payments for street lighting, etc. In general, an increase in dwelling units could result from a shift in use of land from commercial and industrial to residential use. In the case of the Pruitt-Igoe area, the previous nonresidential use of land included large amounts of vacant and industrial land with little or no improvements, such as junk yards. Before acquisition in 1950 the total assessed value of the property was $909,089.[11] At the 1964 tax rate of $4.54 per $100 of assessed valuation, the tax revenue to the city would have been $41,270.[12] There is the problem here concerning what the real estate value of the property would have been in 1964 if public housing had not been put in its place. A real estate selling-price index for areas immediately adjacent to the Pruitt-Igoe project and a comparable area, areas A and A_1 in Table 2-1 indicate that real estate values remained level on the average over the period from 1950 to 1959.[13] In fact, in several of these areas property values declined. This evidence would indicate that the assessed value for 1950 may not be a bad base. Thus, the empirical evidence supports the theoretical assertion that the payments in lieu of taxes are more than twice what the property tax receipts would be from the same area.

A counterargument, however, is that the increased density of the public housing projects caused increased city expenditures for police, fire prevention, and welfare functions. The only evidence on this point is from a statement by Mr. Farris to the Grand Jury of the June Term 1965.[14] This statement presents data on the crime rate in the Fourth Police District, which surrounds the Pruitt-Igoe and Vaughn apartments. The index of crimes excluding "robbery business" and "nonresidential burglary" and the index of crimes against persons in the housing areas is half the rate of the Fourth District. Furthermore, "Since the 1959 Grand Jury Report, it is noteworthy that the incidence of these crimes in Pruitt-Igoe-Vaughn has been reduced to the point that the rate in these Developments is slightly less than the City-wide rate and less than half that for the surrounding areas."[15] Nevertheless, there has been an increased expense required to accomplish this. For police protection the St. Louis Housing Authority has itself had to expend money for a watchman service and equipment. The city police have increased expenditures through their efforts to help train these watchmen.

It is surely true that the occupants "dumped" into these projects are broken families and low-income families of whom many are on public assistance of one kind or another. This does not mean, however, that the housing project is responsible for these expenditures. These expenditures would have been made anyway. Thus, it would seem unreasonable to attribute them to the existence of the housing project.

It may be that the shift of the geographic population distribution in St. Louis might have caused a new need for public facilities. Because of the greater population density a new school and a library may have been constructed. This too cannot be completely attributed to the public housing projects, for the city's public facilities in these areas may have been inadequate even before public housing was constructed. Thus, the increased neighborhood population may have made the need acute enough to warrant new construction.

It was noted in the study described in Chapter 4 that an increased density in the public housing project may cause slum property values to fall in areas from which the tenants came, and may increase the receipts of retail stores in the immediate vicinity of the project, while causing decreases in receipts for establishments in the areas from which the tenants came. On this point the best evidence available is the trend of real estate prices for property before and after construction of public housing. Table 2-1 shows the real estate selling-price index in six areas of St. Louis. Although there is no significant difference in the indexes between areas adjacent to the public housing projects and the comparable areas, all indicate a downward trend in real estate values from 1951 through 1959. This would suggest that the increased density in public housing did not apparently cause much increase in value of property adjacent to public housing for commercial use. If it did, these properties would have tended to increase in value relative to similar areas in other parts of the city. There would, however, seem to be a downward trend in the value of slum property. Certainly part of this is depreciation of these older buildings, but part is a result of the construction boom of the postwar period: The construction of new housing on the periphery of the metropolitan area did cause a reduction in value of the central city units.

Conclusion

It is time to summarize the various shifts in the flow of funds and come to a conclusion about the net shifts in the flow of funds resulting from the construction of the Pruitt-Igoe Housing Projects in St. Louis.

Public housing, and Pruitt-Igoe in particular, have certainly been part of the reason for decreased housing shortages and relief of pressures on slum housing, which are reflected in decreasing property values of slum property. To this extent slum landlords have received relative losses in income.

The low-income families have gained in material goods. It is certainly true that if the subsidy had been given directly to them and they had been allowed to spend it in any way they wished, they would be better off. But the gift in this case is restricted to better housing. Although the tenant's rent expenditures on the average remain the same, they now occupy standard housing. Of the 235 families moving into Pruitt-Igoe from July 1964 to July 1965, at least 163 of the families were moving from substandard housing.[16] The public housing tenants contribute almost nothing toward the public housing subsidy, $0.05 per year per unit. The federal subsidy is around $545 per unit per year.

The taxpayers have lost. They have contributed around $1.5 million each year for the support of these two projects.

Construction workers gained from the shift of resources into construction. The projects did not contribute to the resolution of unemployment because they were built during boom periods.

One of the biggest gainers from the shift of flow of funds has been the city government! They are receiving annually $50,000 to $60,000 more in revenues than if the property remained as slums. Certainly, the present value of this sum over the life of the project more than pays for any share of costs of public facilities caused by location of the project. For example, the present value of $50,000 annual income for 40 years at 3 percent, a low interest rate, would be $1,155,700. The gain to the city would have been half again as much if Pruitt-Igoe had been fully occupied. The city would have received annually $70,000 to $80,000 more in revenues than if the property remained as slums.

Thus, slum landlords and taxpayers have lost, while low income families, construction workers, and the city government have gained. The net effect is indeterminate.

Notes

1. St. Louis Housing Authority, PROJECT FACT SHEET, MO 1-4, and MO 1-5, June 1964.

2. St. Louis Housing Authority, SURVEY OF AREAS FROM WHICH TENANTS ARE DERIVED, January-December 1964.

3. St. Louis Housing Authority, REPORT ON FAMILIES MOVING INTO LOW-RENT HOUSING, MO1-4, MO1-5, July 1964 to July 1965.

4. Hugh O. Nourse, THE EFFECT OF PUBLIC HOUSING ON PROPERTY VALUES IN ST. LOUIS, (Unpublished dissertation, University of Chicago, 1962), p. 23.

5. St. Louis Housing Authority Statement, November 1965.

6. St. Louis POST DISPATCH, February 6, 13, 20, 1966.

7. Hugh O. Nourse, "Redistribution of Income from Public Housing," NATIONAL TAX JOURNAL, vol. 19, no. 11 (March, 1966), p. 17.

8. U.S. Department of Commerce, CONSTRUCTION REVIEW, 1956.

9. ECONOMIC REPORT OF THE PRESIDENT, January 1964, p. 230. Unemployment from 1950 to 1960 was as follows:

Year	Unemployment as Per Cent of Civilian Labor Force
1950	5.3
1951	3.3
1952	3.1
1953	2.9
1954	5.6
1955	4.4
1956	4.2
1957	4.3
1958	6.8
1959	5.5
1960	5.6

10. John C. Bollens, EXPLORING THE METROPOLITAN COMMUNITY (Berkeley: University of California Press, 1961), p. 465.

11. St. Louis Housing Authority Statement.

12. Ibid.

13. Hugh O. Nourse, "The Effect of Public Housing on Property Values in St. Louis," LAND ECONOMICS, vol. 38 (November 1963), p. 439.

14. St. Louis Housing Authority, To the Members of the June Term 1965 Grand Jury, 13 September 1965.

15. Ibid., pp. 4, 5.

16. St. Louis Housing Authority, REPORT ON FAMILIES MOVING INTO LOW-RENT HOUSING, MO 1-4, MO 1-5, July 1964 to July 1965.

6

The Economics of Urban Renewal

" . . . The general welfare and security of the nation and the health and living standards of its people require housing production and related community development sufficient to remedy the serious housing shortage, the elimination of substandard and other inadequate housing through the clearance of slums and blighted areas, and the realization, as soon as possible, of the goal of a decent home and suitable living environment for every American family, thus contributing to the development and redevelopment of communities and to the advancement of the growth, wealth, and security of the nation—" Housing Act of 1949.[1]

To implement the above policy Congress encouraged the establishment of local urban agencies. A local agency could declare an area to be an Urban Renewal Area with the advice and consent of the local and federal governments. The agency would be responsible for initiating action, buying the property, clearing it, and selling it to private interests. Two-thirds of the project cost of federally approved projects would be subsidized by the federal government through direct grants-in-aid.

Two new kinds of assistance from the federal government were established by the Housing Act of 1954. Federal grants became available to help finance public improvements in Urban Renewal Areas. Two-thirds of the cost of such projects as landscaping, expanded recreational and educational facilities, and limited replanning of streets would be subsidized by the federal government. The Act of 1954 also provided for Federal Housing Administration insurance for mortgages secured by rehabilitated or newly constructed properties in the Urban Renewal Area.

In this paper I shall attempt to show that part of the rationale for the urban renewal program is that the benefits of the projects to the community increase property values. This justification for the program, however, is faulty because property values will probably not rise as a result of current policies either to rehabilitate neighborhoods, or to completely rebuild slum areas.

Justification for Urban Renewal

Although our cities had grown and changed without federal assistance prior to 1949, it was felt that it was time to lend a hand, since private enterprise could

Reprinted from LAND ECONOMICS, vol. 42, no. 1 (The University of Wisconsin Press, February 1966).

not provide adequate housing for low-income families. The cost of buying up slum properties, clearing the land, and putting up new structures is greater than the value of the new structures. If it is not profitable for private enterprise, what is the justification for government assistance? It was said that slums or blighted areas create costs to the community. Property values decline, fire and police protection costs increase, and public health and welfare costs increase because the unhealthful surroundings breed disease and crime.[2] Several studies, however, have shown that improved housing does not have many of the social benefits initially attributed to it.[3] Nevertheless, since reduction of these costs through renewal would accrue to the community rather than the individual owner or builder, government assistance would be necessary. The government should be willing to incur additional expense because of the additional social benefits the community receives. In economic terms the subsidy must be equivalent, or thought to be equivalent, to the social benefits (or reduction of social costs), or the community would not assent to the projects.

Any subsidy, however, must be financed. If it is financed through taxation, it represents a shift of income from the taxed to the subsidized. In this paper I shall neglect any social costs that may be created by the financing scheme. If there are no external benefits, as will be suggested in this paper, urban renewal becomes an instrument for redistributing income, or for improving houses to a certain standard determined by the community. As A.H. Schaaf writes, "Quantitative determination of the benefits of urban renewal is most complex and probably can at best represent only tenuous approximations."[4] Therefore, he says that we should try to find the least cost means of improving neighborhoods to the given standard. If redistribution of income, or raising housing standards is the aim of the community, there may be more efficient ways to do it. This may be a fruitful direction for further research.

Of course, there is another reason for government intervention. If one owner in a blighted area improved his property, the value of the property would not increase because the neighborhood itself had not changed. It might be profitable to improve the property if all owners simultaneously rehabilitated their property, improving the whole neighborhood. In this case some form of government coercion might be all that is necessary.

Davis and Whinston have taken this as the real problem of blight. "Blight is said to exist whenever (1) strictly individual action does not result in redevelopment, (2) the coordination of decision-making via some means would result in redevelopment, and (3) the sum of benefits from renewal could exceed the sum of costs."[5] If blight is defined in this way, there is no reason for the federal government to subsidize urban renewal. If the only obstacle to renewal is the inability of neighborhood owners to cooperate in order to renew the use of land to its more profitable use, either building code enforcement, or condemnation of the property through the community power of eminent domain, would be the only tools necessary to get a project completed. If the project is profitable, there would be no need for a government subsidy.

Davis and Whinston point out, however, that this definition of blight would call for the renewal of some areas not including poor housing, and could exclude areas that do include poor housing.[6] They conceive of urban renewal as a device for reallocating resources to their more profitable use, and it may very well be that slum housing is the most profitable use of some land. They suggest that poor housing is a result of families with poor income, and that the most efficient way to improve their housing is to redistribute income. through a taxing of the well-to-do in order to transfer income to poorer families. Poor people could be made better off by a subsidy of money rather than housing, but the increased income might not be spent for improved housing. In any case, the community through Congress has decided to redistribute income by improving housing, even if it might cost more than a redistribution of income.

Effects of Urban Renewal on Property Values

If public improvements make a neighborhood or community a more desirable place to live, the benefits may be reflected in part through higher land values in the area surrounding the improvement. Indeed, this argument has been used to defend renewal. Donald H. Webster has written that "the appropriation of public funds for clearing areas for private redevelopment can be justified in part as a penalty that the community must pay for past errors and in part as an investment which will eventually be repaid from the higher tax values created."[7] Since real property value changes are the economic effects of urban renewal projects that I am studying in this paper, the next step in our analysis is to study the likely effects of various kinds of urban renewal projects upon property values in the project and in adjacent areas.

The question hinges upon the determinants of property value. For any one property there can be one or more ceiling prices and a floor price. The ceiling price is the maximum amount that a firm or individual is willing to pay for a property. It is the discounted value of the future annual net income that he anticipates from the use of the property. The discount rate (interest rate) is the one that he can get on alternative outlays with equal risk, since he will invest in the enterprise from which he expects to get the most return. Similarly, the floor price is the minimum amount that a firm or individual is willing to accept for a property.[8]

The receipts in determining the net return are the rents that a buyer would expect to obtain if he owned the property, the rent an occupier would be willing to pay rather than move or, in the case of a developer, the price the property will bring upon development. The costs that would be subtracted from these receipts to obtain a net return are maintenance, provision of services, taxes, and depreciation in the case of a terminable interest in the property.

At this point it would be a good idea to observe that building cost does not wholly determine the value of a property. If a person were to build a property he would certainly not spend more on construction than the discounted value of the annual net returns that he could earn from the use of the property. This, however, is a different situation than a government that has invested in property without regard to the discounted value of the annual net returns, or an individual subsidized for part of his outlays. The subsidized individual will tend to overbuild. His own outlays will cover the present value of the annual net incomes to be earned from the property, but the funds given to him through subsidy will be in excess of this figure so that the community's outlay exceeds the present value of the net annual returns of the property. The market price of the property will fall short of the construction cost but will be between the floor and ceiling prices previously described.

We can divide the urban renewal programs into five groups for the purpose of studying their impact on property values. Within a narrow view urban renewal projects could influence property values two ways. First, the value of the blocks cleared and rebuilt may change. Second, environmental improvements may influence the values of the blocks improved and the values of the surrounding properties. The former type of renewal is excluded as an environmental improvement because these projects usually include complete neighborhoods. Their boundaries often coincide with natural boundaries, such as railroad right-of-ways, so that changes in the character of the neighborhood have little impact on adjacent neighborhoods. As it now stands, however, current policy also includes rehabilitation of neighborhoods through building code enforcement, public improvement, and liberal financing. Therefore, we must include two more potential sources of influence on property value: building code enforcement and liberal financing. The fifth influence is that of the combination of segregation and complete clearance renewal.

Influence on Value of Cleared Area

Merely because new buildings have replaced older ones will not cause an area to have a higher value. If the renewal changes the occupants of a previous slum area from low-income to high-income persons or businesses, values will increase, particularly if the location is very suitable for the new use, and these persons are willing to pay more for the site. But is there a net gain to the community? The crucial point is what has happened to the previous poor occupants. They have been forced out of their homes and businesses. Perhaps there is a gain to the community, if they decide to spend more of their incomes for housing. Still, one suspects that when they are faced with alternative choices, all of which cost more than their current housing, there will be a tendency for doubling-up of families. This was a common experience among all families during the Depression of the 1930s when family incomes were reduced.

Property values would change depending upon the degree of doubling up, all other things remaining equal. Specifically, the analysis assumes a shift in population location without any population growth. If some percent increase in rent would cause the same percent reduction in the amount of housing used by slum dwellers because of doubling up of families, or because of their purchases of smaller living areas, there would be no change in total value. If the rent increase caused a greater percentage decrease in the amount of housing used by the former slum dwellers, property values would tend to decline. On the other hand, if the rent increase caused a smaller percentage reduction in the amount of housing used, the property values would tend to rise. A recent study by Richard F. Muth suggests that the first case is right.[9] Therefore, there will most likely be no change in property values.

The notion that renewal of the complete clearance type merely shifts slums around implies that slums are due to the poverty of people and that this class of person will always be with us. To me this has been provocatively set forth by Charles J. Stokes. In an article, "A Theory of Slums," he outlines a taxonomy of slums which includes four types.[10] The classes are generated from two variables. "One is the psychological attitude toward the possibility of success in moving up through the class structure by assimilation or acculturation to full participation in the economic and social life of the community. The other is a measure of socio-economic handicaps and barriers to such movement."[11] Thus, we can distinguish intuitively between those slums in which people intend to better themselves and believe they have a chance, or *hope*, of success, and those slums in which people do not intend to better themselves, or *despair* because they do not think that they have a chance to better themselves. We can also distinguish between that group of people or class who can move up through the class structure (escalator class) and those who cannot (non-escalator).

The four kinds of slum dwellers can be labeled in the following manner: (A) people who have hope and belong to an escalator class; (B) people who despair and belong to an escalator class; (C) people who have hope but who belong to a non-escalator class, and (D) people who despair and who belong to a non-escalator class. This sort of taxonomy would be interesting, but out of place in this paper if this were as far as we could take the analysis. There are implications, however, which make it useful for our purposes. Newly arriving immigrants with ability to learn the trades, skills, language and culture of a community, and who belong to an escalator class may settle in the city. As the economy grows and expands, it will absorb these people. The size of such a neighborhood within the community depends upon the relative growth rates of the economy, the need for additional workers, and the rate of immigration into the community. The slum will grow if higher wages and job opportunities attract more immigrants than there are job opportunities. The slum will contract as the immigration slows down and growth of the community absorbs more persons into good jobs.

Curiously the slum dominated by the type C dweller also tends to contract

with economic progress. Due to caste or escalator barriers to those of a particular class and, in spite of ability, these people are not integrated in the community. Nevertheless, they better themselves within their own neighborhood, building better homes, and neighborhoods, as they increase in wealth. Still, their progress will not be as fast as it would be if they were integrated into the community.

The slums inhabited by persons of types B and D will tend to expand. Professor Stokes concludes that slums persist as the economy grows because the work requirements and skills increase and at the same time workers' pay is distributed more in accordance with ability. Caste barriers reinforce that of ability and are also forces for the continuation of slums.

Therefore it is likely that slums will persist with economic growth of the community. Although renewal might attract industry and create new employment opportunities, slums would persist. The specific influence that an urban renewal project of the complete clearance type will have on total property values in the city depends upon the reaction of the project neighborhood's former occupants to increased rents. Nevertheless, if the worst housing in the city has been torn down, only better housing is left. The quality of the total stock of housing has been improved. The question remains, however, whether denser use and slum dweller use will cause reduction in quality.

Environmental Influence

Although it has often been said that public housing and urban renewal projects, such as parks, schools, community buildings, etc., would enhance the neighborhood property values and thus increase the taxable base of the city, nothing much has been done to test these speculations with empirical studies. The one exception has been the studies to estimate the influence of improved streets and highways on property values. Property values adjacent to new street or highway improvements may increase or diminish depending upon the type of improvement. A limited access highway may diminish values adjacent to the highway while it may increase property values located farther from the city but not immediately adjacent to the improvement. A recent study, however, has made the point that these increases in value may not be net increases to the community. By shifting traffic from other streets, this improvement may cause decreases in value along other streets of the community.[12]

I have made one attempt to see whether public housing has an effect on the property values in the surrounding neighborhood. The trends of the prices of property in the neighborhoods surrounding St. Louis public housing projects were compared with the trends in other neighborhoods with the same social and economic characteristics. The price data were estimated from the amount of tax stamps affixed to deeds at the time of sale of the property. The price trends covered the period, 1937-1959, beginning before the projects were considered and terminating several years after the completion of almost all of the projects. My study suggests that public housing had no influence on property values in the surrounding neighborhood immediately adjacent to the public housing projects.[13] Further studies need to be made, however, to investigate the effect of different kinds of public improvements on property values so that public policy might be guided more by facts than conjecture.

Influence of Building Code Enforcement

In the first place, property owners would have complied with the building code standards before enforcement if they could cooperate with each other and if the expected value after compliance were greater than its current value plus the cost of compliance. Values after compliance will rise, perhaps to this level, if the demand should increase as a result of the more desirable physical dwellings. As before, this must mean, however, that families currently living in these dwellings must spend a greater proportion of their income on housing, that higher-income residents who will pay the higher rents and values have moved into the neighborhood, or that those currently living in the neighborhood will occupy a smaller amount of space. This last may be impossible if it violates the occupancy standards of the housing code. If the income of the neighborhood does not change and greater doubling up is not allowed, then values will not be likely to increase.

If values would not rise above the value of the property before code compliance plus the cost of compliance, could code enforcement still raise housing standards? Let us assume that there are no alternatives for the people currently living in these houses. We shall also assume that the code is strictly enforced. With the new constraint, owners will comply with the code so long as the after value of the property is greater than the cost of the code compliance. Thus, renewal *may* take place even if no change should take place in values.

One might want to argue, however, that these residences with improved quality will increase in rent because they are now in the same market as other good quality housing. This is not true. Housing of the same quality, but different in location, may differ in desirability and thus receive different rents. The location factors are the neighborhood influences of schools, churches, shopping centers, congestion, industrial location, population characteristics and distance from the Central Business District.

Influence of Liberal Financing

The current Housing Act also provides for the federal encouragement of rehabilitation through insurance on mortgages with liberal terms for the purpose of rehabilitation of old houses, or building new houses in an urban renewal area. This has the interesting economic effect of not changing the rent levels but perhaps still causing some increase in property values.[14] We can consider the income stream from the property as the flow of funds available for financing the improvement of the asset. The price of this income stream depends as much upon the interest rate as upon the actual level of annual income. The lower the interest rate, the greater will be the price of the income flow. Thus, the lower the interest rate, the greater will be the amount of capital that can be obtained on the basis of a given income stream. Liberal financing will tend to increase the after-renewal values and encourage more persons to renovate since more properties will have after-renewal values greater than renewal costs. Schaaf gives tentative estimates for the magnitude of the increase in values by analyzing income multipliers.[15]

As a rule of thumb, the value of a property can be estimated as a multiple of the net annual income exclusive of mortgage payments and return to the owner. For example, assume that the investor wants the return of his equity in 5 years, so that 20 percent of the equity is returned each year. A 25-year, 5.5 percent interest loan amounting to 90 percent of the total property value can be obtained. Then the annual return necessary to pay the return to equity, interest of debt and reduction of mortgage would be 8.66 percent of the total property value. This could be calculated in the following way: Annual return to equity: 20 percent of 10 percent of the property value, 2%. Interest and principal on mortgage, 6.6%—total 8.6%. In order for there to be an annual return of 8.6 percent, the purchase price must be 11.5 times the annual income.

On the basis of current mortgage financing terms the income multipliers range from four to seven. This is calculated on the basis of two extreme but typical cases. In each case the price of the property is $10,000 and the buyer will make a down payment of $1,000 and borrow the rest. In the first case the buyer obtains a first mortgage of $7,000 to be paid off in 15 years with an interest rate of 6 percent and a second mortgage of $2,222 to be paid off in 5 years with an interest rate of 8 percent. Since the second mortgage is discounted, the buyer only receives $2,000. The total annual payout requirement can be calculated as follows:

Annual return to equity: return of equity in 5 years	$ 200
Interest and principal on first mortgage each year	557
Interest and principal on second mortgage each year	721
Total annual payout requirement	$1,478

The multiplier in this case is 6.8. The price is approximately 6.8 times the necessary annual net income.

In the second case the buyer obtains a first mortgage of $5,000 to be paid off in 10 years with an interest rate of 8 percent and a second mortgage of $5,715 to be paid off in 5 years with an interest rate of 8 percent. Since the second mortgage is discounted, the buyer only receives $4,000. The total annual payout requirement can be calculated as follows:

Annual return to equity: return of equity in 5 years	$ 200
Interest and principal on first mortgage each year	745
Interest and principal on second mortgage each year	1,431
Total annual payout requirement	$2,376

The multiplier in this case is 4.2. The price is approximately 4.2 times the necessary annual net income.

Schaaf estimates the impact of the liberal financing to be an increase in the income multipler to 11. He assumes that liberal financing might enable buyers or renovators to obtain 25-year mortgages with an interest rate of 5.75 percent on 90 percent of the property value. To pay off the interest and principal on such a loan, the buyer would need a return of 7 percent each year in addition to the 2 percent required for return of his equity. Therefore, the required net annual income would have to be 9 percent. In order for any given income stream to be 9 percent of the property price, the price must equal 11 times the annual income. An increase of the multiplier from 7 to 11 would imply that a property with a net annual income stream of $1,000 would increase in value from $7,000 to $11,000.

There are several problems to be considered before the above argument is accepted. In the first place the relevant interest rate for translating an income stream into a capital value is that interest return that the investor can earn on alternative investments. Therefore, if the government-insured loans must be provided at interest rates below those that private lenders can obtain elsewhere at comparable risk, lenders will not provide the necessary funds. Thus, arbitrarily depressing interest rates will increase the amount of mortgage money sought by home owners to rehabilitate their property but at the same time it will decrease the amount of money made available by lenders unless some provision is made for government support of additional credit.

This leads to a second problem. The increase in credit may lead to inflation of prices. This could cause an increase in the cost of rehabilitation. It seems reasonable to assume, however, that the renewal market is so small a share of the construction materials market that there would be no inflation.

Finally, there is the borrower's position. In the slum or blighted area very few will own their houses unencumbered by a mortgage. In fact, one urban renewal study has shown that this was a major obstacle to lending for rehabilitation of a neighborhood.[16]

Influence of Segregation

Since incomes from property are unlikely to change if the land of an urban renewal area is used for low-income housing, redevelopers may find construction of housing for the former residents an unprofitable undertaking even if land values are subsidized and mortgages insured. Thus, renewal has often meant changing neighborhood characteristics by building for higher-income families, rolling back segregated boundaries, or building industrial and commercial properties.

One suspects that urban renewal often takes place in order to change the boundary of housing segregation. Martin J. Bailey has indicated the economics of such a situation.[17] The principles can be explained by looking at an hypothetical and simplified case. In the first place, a boundary problem occurs only when one set of persons is repelled by another, but the feeling is not mutual. If the feeling is mutual, the two groups would not be adjacent. Suppose that there are two groups of people, X and Y. The X people prefer to live next to Y people rather than next to X people. There is an area with similar property and equal-sized lots divided by eight parallel streets, A through H. Streets A through D are occupied by group X; streets E through H are occupied by group Y. The effect of the proximity of the two groups to each other will be limited to streets D and E. Prices along street D will be higher than for other X-occupied housing while prices along street E will be lower than for other Y-occupied housing. The persons of X group prefer to live near the Y group and therefore are willing to pay a premium to do so. People in the Y group prefer to live near others of their own group rather than to live near those of X group and therefore pay less to live in properties adjacent to the X group on street E.

Suppose that the X group is composed of non-white persons and the Y group is composed of white persons. Under what conditions does block-busting become profitable? Non-white occupancy will expand when the price per unit of their houses plus the premium for living near the Y group is greater than the price per unit of Y-group housing less the discount for living near non-whites. Expansion of the non-white group will continue until these two sums are equal.

The second question to ask ourselves is under what circumstances it is worthwhile from the community standpoint to roll back an expansion of the non-white or X group? We will start with the assumption that the community will be better off, the greater is the sum of its property values. Therefore, it becomes profitable to roll back an expansion of the non-white group only if the property values of that group per unit of housing, without the premium, is less than the prices of houses in the all white group. Thus, if the minority groups of our cities are occupying housing priced higher for the same space and quality of housing, the welfare of the community will be greater if the higher priced property expands and is not contracted. From the community's point of view the boundary is in equilibrium when no change in the total value of property will take place, if the boundary is moved. This will occur when the price of X-group housing is equal to the price of Y-group housing. If X-house prices are equal to Y-house prices, a movement of the boundary will simply remove the premium from one block while adding it to another, and remove the discount from one block while subtracting it from another. Therefore, if equal housing is priced higher for non-white occupancy than for white occupancy, urban renewal should not roll back such a boundary.

Conclusion

In conclusion, the purpose of the urban renewal program has been to remove slums and improve housing. The justification for the program has often been that the social benefits from the program would improve values and increase local taxes. To renew for poor people will most probably not result in increased land or property values. Redevelopers and planners have often recognized that private persons, even with the subsidy, could not build new housing for the prior slum dwellers for a profit. As a result the projects have been for higher income families, rolling back segregation boundaries, or the building of commercial and industrial properties. As I have tried to show, under certain conditions, changing racial characteristics of the neighborhood may lower aggregate community property values while redeveloping the land for a higher and more profitable use may not and should not need a government subsidy. More importantly, it may result in a shift of the slums to a new location. Therefore, if we are to give attention to the purpose of Congress, we should recommend refocusing attention on other forms of housing subsidy to attain "the goal of a decent home, and suitable living environment for every American family."

Notes

1. Public Law 171, 81st Congress, S. 1070, Housing Act of 1949.
2. For one typical description of these costs see, Donald H. Webster, URBAN PLANNING AND MUNICIPAL PUBLIC POLICY (New York, New York, Harper & Brothers, 1958), pp. 494-497.
3. John P. Dean, "The Myths of Housing Reform," AMERICAN SOCIO-LOGICAL REVIEW (April 1949), pp. 281-288; Daniel M. Wilner, Rosabelle Price Walkely, Marvin N. Glasser and Mathew Taybeck, "The Effect of Housing Quality on Morbidity," Preliminary Findings of the Johns Hopkins Longitudinal Study, AMERICAN JOURNAL OF PUBLIC HEALTH (December 1958), pp. 1607-1615.
4. A.H. Schaaf, ECONOMIC ASPECTS OF URBAN RENEWAL: THEORY POLICY AND AREA ANALYSIS, Real Estate Research Program, Institute of

Business and Economic Research Report 14 (University of California, 1960), p. 5.

5. Otto A. Davis and Andrew B. Whinston, "The Economics of Urban Renewal," LAW AND CONTEMPORARY PROBLEMS (Winter 1961), p. 105.

6. Ibid., p. 105.

7. Donald H. Webster, op. cit., p. 496.

8. For a discussion of the determinants of urban property value, see Ralph Turvey, THE ECONOMICS OF REAL PROPERTY (London, George Allen and Unwin, Ltd., 1957), Chapter 2.

9. Richard F. Muth, "The Demand for Non-Farm Housing," THE DEMAND FOR DURABLE GOODS, Arnold C. Harberger, ed., (Chicago, University of Chicago, 1960).

10. Charles J. Stokes, "A Theory of Slums," LAND ECONOMICS (August 1962), pp. 187-197.

11. Ibid., p. 188.

12. Herbert Mohring, "Land Values and the Measurement of Highway Benefits," JOURNAL OF POLITICAL ECONOMY (June 1961), pp. 236-249.

13. Hugh O. Nourse, "The Effect of Public Housing on Property Values in St. Louis," LAND ECONOMICS (November 1963), pp. 433-441.

14. Schaaf, op. cit., p. 15.

15. Ibid., p. 22. The figures that follow were taken directly from this source.

16. RENEWAL AND REVENUE, An Evaluation of the Urban Renewal Program in Detroit, Michigan: Chapters 6 and 7.

17. Martin J. Bailey, "Note on the Economics of Residential Zoning and Urban Renewal," LAND ECONOMICS (August 1959), pp. 288-292.

7

The Effect of Air Pollution on House Values

It has often been said that air pollution will have a detrimental effect on residential property values. For example, Alfred Marshall had this to say about urban air pollution:

But the case of high site values is that concentration of population, which is threatening a scarcity of fresh air and light and playroom so grievous as to lower the vigour and the joyousness of the rising generation. Thus rich private gains accrue, not merely through causes which are public rather than private in character, but also at the expense of one of the chief forms of public wealth.

In regard to site values, it would seem well to rule that all land, whether technically urban or not, should be regarded as having a special site value if when cleared of buildings it could be sold at even a moderately high price, say £200 an acre. It might then be subjected to a general rate assessed on its capital value; and, in addition, to a "fresh air rate" to be spent by local authority under full central control for the purposes indicated above. This fresh air rate would not be a very heavy burden on owners, for a good deal of it would be returned to them in the form of higher values for those building sites which remained.[1]

The evidence, however, is quite skimpy. Urban land economists and real estate appraisers have from time to time made general comments that nuisances, including air pollution, made a neighborhood a less desirable place to live. One of the first analysts of urban land to write was a mortgage banker, Richard M. Hurd. He had the following comment to make upon residential land use:

On the other hand, the basis of residence values is social and not economic—even though the land goes to the highest bidder—the rich selecting the locations which please them, those of moderate means living as near as possible, and so on down the scale of wealth, the poorest workmen taking the final leavings, either adjacent to such nuisances as factories, railroads, docks, etc., or far out of the city. Certain features appear to attract the wealthy in selecting their residence districts, among these being nearness to parks, a good approach from the business centre, not too near nor yet too far, a moderate elevation if obtainable, favorable transportation facilities, despite the fact that the rich ride in their own carriages and automobiles, and above all absence of nuisances.[2]

This statement needs but little rewriting to represent current knowledge about residential housing values and location. Later the urban land economist, Richard U. Ratcliff, after describing other factors affecting the location of housing made the following comment on nuisances:

Source: Reprinted from LAND ECONOMICS, vol. 42, no. 2 (The University of Wisconsin Press, May 1966).

Another desirable feature of residential locations is the absence of obnoxious land uses or unwelcome social groups, together with some protection against the invasion of such uses or groups. Thus neighborhoods protected by adequate zoning regulations or deed restrictions are favored.[3]

Currently, the American Institute of Real Estate Appraisers' *Real Estate Appraising*, a textbook on how to estimate the value of property, makes the following points on the impact of such things as air pollution on a residential neighborhood.

A neighborhood's exposure to odors, smoke, dust, and noise from commercial or manufacturing enterprises limits its desirability. The physical presence of a nuisance depreciates the value of a home which is located, for instance, across the street from a tavern. Some areas are liable to hazards such as the possibility of floods, landslides, air accidents, or perhaps so common a problem as an undue volume of automobile or truck traffic. Not every such hazard is readily apparent; but the possible existence of any such threat to value should not escape the appraiser.[4]

These judgments, however, are a result of general observation of the real estate market rather than any attempt to statistically estimate the extent of damage caused to values by air pollution. This paper is a theoretical analysis of how to measure the direct impact that air pollution has upon property values. It was developed as a result of attempts to estimate this impact in a more extensive study to estimate the social costs of air pollution not incurred by firms causing the pollution. In the final section of the paper the results of the statistical studies will be presented.[5]

Theory of Urban House Values

Several recent theories of urban land use have postulated a flat plain with equal transportation costs per mile in all directions from some central market. The ideal allocation of the available space among uses is determined instantaneously.[6] This approach is useful for many problems. Nevertheless, one of the most important aspects of urban real estate property is its durability. As circumstances change it is not economical to immediately tear down all the buildings that do not represent the highest and best use of the site on which they are located. The land use pattern of a city changes only slowly to the changing transportation network, population, and income of the community. A building will not be torn down until the value of the land and building plus the cost of tearing down the old building and constructing the new one are less than the present discounted value of the expected earnings from the new use.

In any one year the amount of new housing made available to the population is small relative to the currently old, but available stock of housing. There were about 661,000 houses in the St. Louis Metropolitan Area in 1960. From January 1950 to March 1960 about 18,000 new units were added, on the average, each year to the stock for an addition of about 3 percent per year.[7] Thus, at any given time the choice of housing available to the urban population is fixed. The number of structures is relatively fixed, some structures are single-family and some are apartments. Their location in the city depends upon the transportation and job conditions existing at the time of construction or remodeling. The economic problem of allocation is then who is to occupy which house. This will depend upon demand conditions. It will depend upon the income, tastes, and occupations of the households. The households willing and able to pay the most for each house will occupy it. If there should be a shortage, some may be left out, or forced to double-up but prices will rise sufficiently above construction costs to encourage new building. If there is a glut, vacancies will rise, prices will fall, and no new construction will take place.

One way of looking at the determination of housing values in the short run is to array the houses of the city from the worst to the best. But what do we mean by worst and best? We understand this to be the attributes of a house that make people demand it. One of the most important features making a house desirable is access to stores, entertainment, church and schools, but primarily access to job. The theories of urban land use mentioned at the beginning of this section have made job access the primary motive for household location. Its implication that population density increases near major centers of employment has been verified in several studies of the city.[8] This would suggest that higher income households would live closest to work and poorer families farther from work. But journey to work studies suggest the opposite.[9] The wealthier are willing to make a longer journey to work. This would seem to indicate, as Hurd suggests in the quotation at the beginning of this paper, that job-access may be a limiting factor in residential demand. Job access limits how far away from the job it is possible to locate. Within a thirty or forty minute driving range of work, the household selects a house according to its amenities. We can neglect the access of houses and apartments to stores, schools and churches since these activities follow the concentrations of population.

The amenities that make a house desirable are absence of noise and dirt, the economic and social characteristics of one's neighbors and the family stage of one's neighbors. The final two characteristics suggest that households wish to live near other similar households. Desirable neighborhoods are homogeneous, and most neighborhoods are homogeneous with respect to income, occupation, and family stage.[10] Thus, we can legitimately speak of neighborhoods rather than individual houses and consider the determinates of the average property value in a neighborhood.

Of course we have neglected the size of houses. All other things remaining equal, such as income and occupation, the smaller a house the less will be paid for it. Once the houses are arrayed from the worst to the best, the value of each is determined by who is willing to pay the most for each since that household will occupy it. Perhaps the theory can be made clearer with a hypothetical example taken from Wallace F. Smith.[11] Tables 7-1 through 7-3 are taken directly from the monograph by Smith. The rest of the analysis is my own adaptation. In Table 7-1, array the houses of a community from A through E, from the worst in quality to the best in quality where quality represents degrees of fresh air. These are the only five houses in the community. To simplify the problem assume the houses are all of the same size. There are also five families or households of the same size and occupation that are to live in these houses. They earn different incomes. The households are numbered from 1 through 5. One can also consider these five families as five homogeneous groups of families and the five houses as five homogeneous groups of houses, the groups being equal in size to each other. The first family earns the lowest income, the second family earns more, and the fifth family earns the highest income. The lowest amount in rent that any family is willing to pay is L by household 1 for the lowest quality house. For better quality housing household one will pay more. According to the hypothetical example the household will be willing to pay 5 more dollars for each increase in quality. The rent offer is a monthly rent figure that can be converted into a property value figure by capitalizing the rent income at the market rate of interest.

Furthermore, as household income increases the family is willing to pay more

Table 7-1

			Houses		
Households	A	B	C	D	E
1	L	5	10	15	20
2	10	–	–	–	–
3	20	–	–	–	–
4	30	–	–	–	–
5	40	–	–	–	–

Table 7-2

			Houses		
Households	A	B	C	D	E
1					
2		1	2	3	4
3		2	4	6	8
4		3	6	9	12
5		4	8	12	16

Table 7-3

	Houses				
Households	A	B	C	D	E
1	L	5	10	15	20
2	10	16	22	28	34
3	20	27	34	41	48
4	30	38	46	54	62
5	40	49	58	67	76

for the same quality house. This is illustrated by the column of offers for quality A house. Each increase in income brings out an additional offer of 10 more dollars. To fill in the rest of the table with only the given data would imply that household 2, with more income than household 1, would pay $L + 15$ for house B and would pay no more for the increase in quality than family 1. It would seem more realistic that quality would have some income elasticity and that family 2 would pay more for the increase in quality than family 1. Additional amounts that might be offered for increased quality by each level of family income are shown in Table 7-2.

In Table 7-3 we combine the two previous tables in order to find out the offers that each family will make for each quality of house. The market solution to the allocation of the five houses among the five families is that the fifth family is the highest bidder for the best house. Family 4 is the highest bidder for the next best house, etc. Thus, the diagonal of the matrix in Table 7-3 shows the market value for each house. The market solution yields the highest total rent.[a]

When we observe the market we see five houses, each with a value as indicated by the diagonal of the above matrix. A regression analysis with property value as the dependent value and income and quality as the independent values, will show a significant relationship between income and value, or between quality and value. The observed relationship between quality and value will indicate both the income and price effect of quality. The observed

Value	Income	Quality
L	1	A
L +16	2	B
L +34	3	C
L +54	4	D
L +76	5	E

[a]One might argue that the diagonal yields the *maximum* possible rents. In this example there is room for bargaining. The best house could be valued from $L + 63$ to $L + 76$ and still be occupied by household 5. If we think of the 661,000 families in the metropolitan area arrayed by income, the differences between offers would be smaller.

relationship with income will be too strong because it will also include the price elasticity between value and quality. If income and quality are both used as independent variables, levels of air pollution may show no association with value because income absorbs all of the variation. Nevertheless the households with high income live in neighborhoods devoid of pollution and their rent reflects it.

If families with the same level of income must choose between houses with fresh air and those without, we may catch the association in the regression equation. The hypothetical demand matrix might look as in Table 7-4 in which families 3 and 4 have the same income. In this case the difference in value between houses C and D would be between $L + 34$ and $L + 41$ and would be solely due to the difference in quality. Nevertheless, even if a single equation regression estimate is possible to calculate, only a single value will be attached to quality. A regression coefficient of quality will show the change in price for different qualities, given income, but the coefficient will indicate the same change in offers for the same different qualities for different income levels. The income elasticity of demand for quality would by implication be assumed to be zero.

Another way to attack the problem would be to find a specific instance in which the air quality of a place within a city changed and observe the impact on property values. In the following illustration we will apply the matrix demand approach to a case in which the quality of one house changes.

Once again assume that there are five families, 1 through 5, with increasing levels of income and five houses, A through E, with increasing levels of fresh air. Furthermore, assume that the offers for houses are as shown in Table 7-3. For some reason, perhaps the location of a paint plant, the air quality of house C falls to that of house B. The demand matrix would then change so that the offers for house C were the same as those for house B. The demand matrix might appear as in Table 7-5. By comparing Table 7-3, the situation before the change in pollution, to Table 7-5 we find that house C would fall in value from $L + 34$ to $L + 27$ as a result of the reduction in its quality from the air pollution. This difference is a measure of the value attached to the air pollution.

Consider a case in which the change in pollution occurs simultaneously with

Table 7-4

Households	Houses				
	A	B	C	D	E
1	L	5	10	15	20
2	10	16	22	28	34
3	20	27	34	41	48
4	20	27	34	41	48
5	40	49	58	67	76

69

Table 7-5

		Houses			
Households	A	B	C	D	E
1	L	5	5	15	20
2	10	16	16	28	34
3	20	27	27	41	48
4	30	38	38	54	62
5	40	49	49	67	76

an increase in households and houses. Add a house of the same quality as D and call it D′, and add a family with income 3 and call it family 3′. From the relationships previously postulated we can once again construct a new demand matrix, Table 7-6: In this hypothetical case family 4 moves into the new house D′. Family 3′, the new family, moves into house D but its value falls to $L + 41$ from $L + 54$ since no family with a higher income makes an offer for the house. Once again house C, the house with the change in air quality, falls in value from $L + 34$ to $L + 27$, and the difference is totally due to air pollution.

Suppose, however, that the new family had had an income equal to that of family 2. The income distribution of the population had changed so that family 3 could move up and out of the polluted house C to a better house D. To see this we can construct the following Table 7-7 in the same way as Table 7-6. Instead of increasing families of income 3, however, we show two offers for each quality house at the income 2. Family 4 moves up to the new housing D′ by offering $L + 54$; family 3 moves up to house D by offering $L + 41$; and the two families at income level 2 offer the same for houses B and C since they have been reduced to the same quality by air pollution. The final result, comparing Table 7-7 to Table 7-3, is that the value of C falls from $L + 34$ to $L + 16$. The difference in the value of house C cannot be completely attributed to the change in quality. Part of the reduction in value is a result of new housing that made it possible for the previous higher income occupants of house C to move to better

Table 7-6

		Houses				
Households	A	B	C	D	D'	E
1	L	5	5	15	15	20
2	10	16	16	28	28	34
3	20	27	27	41	41	48
3'	20	27	27	41	41	48
4	30	38	38	54	54	62
5	40	49	49	67	67	76

Table 7-7

Households	Houses					
	A	B	C	D	D'	E
1	L	5	5	15	15	20
2	10	16	16	28	28	34
2'	10	16	16	28	28	34
3	20	27	27	41	41	48
4	30	38	38	54	54	62
5	40	49	49	67	67	76

quality housing. Thus, one has to take account of the income of families in a neighborhood affected by air pollution before attributing the whole decline of price, if there is one, to air pollution.

The implication of this analysis for empirical studies of the economic impact of air pollution on house values is that only estimates of the price effect catch the psychic and increased maintenance costs of air pollution. When income effects are introduced, statistical estimates of the impact of air pollution on property value may reflect changes in income distribution, as well as in increased air pollution.

Statistical Estimates of the Impact of Air Pollution on House Values in St. Louis

In a recent study of the economic costs of air pollution a cross-sectional and time series analysis were made of the impact of air pollution on property values in St. Louis.[12] In the cross-sectional study the difficulty of obtaining data on each individual house and household and the multitudinous taste variables was overcome by using neighborhood data. Taking the St. Louis Metropolitan Area in 1960 as a case study, the difference between neighborhoods in the average property values of single-family dwellings was explained by a regression equation including twelve independent variables.[13] Since neighborhoods tend to be homogeneous with respect to income and other socio-economic variables, idiosyncrasies of households and structures would tend to wash out, using the neighborhood data. Neighborhoods were defined as census tracts because they were the most convenient to use and because it was assumed that they were sufficiently homogeneous with respect to the variables relevant for the study.

The independent variables in the regression equation were an index of air pollution, median number of rooms, percent of all housing units built from January 1950 to March 1960, houses per square mile, distance in time from the Central Business District, accessibility to major through streets, school quality, percent of workers in blue collar occupations, persons per unit, percent of units occupied by non-whites, a dummy variable indicating whether the tract was in Illinois or Missouri to account for differences in property taxes, and median family income in 1959. The regression coefficients of all but the school quality variable turned out to be significantly different from zero at the 0.05 level of significance (two-tail test). About 94 percent of the variation in property values was explained. The index of air pollution was based on milligrams of sulfur trioxide per square centimeter per day averaged for one year. The regression coefficient of the air pollution variable indicated values were $245 less for every increase of 0.5 milligrams sulfur trioxide per 100 square centimeters per day, *ceteris paribus*. One of the variables held constant was income. Thus, this estimate is a weighted average of the price difference offered for cleaner air. For low income levels the differential for cleaner air would be expected to be less; for high income levels the differential for cleaner air would be expected to be higher. This coefficient would change with changes in income distribution, whether air pollution changed or not.

The time series study was an analysis of property values in one neighborhood in St. Louis. During 1962 residents of a quiet, middle-class neighborhood in south St. Louis began to complain about the choking gases emitted from a plant that had just been taken over by a metal fabricating firm. The odors were described as nauseous, causing "headaches, smarting of the eyes and injury to the respiratory system and loss of appetite."[14] Prior to that time there had been no complaints about the quality of air in the neighborhood although 17 percent of the census tract acreage in which the neighborhood is located had been devoted to industrial use for many years.

To assess the effect that pollution had on property values in this neighborhood apart from changes in general market conditions that occur over time, a control area which was as similar to the affected area as possible was selected. Indices of recorded sales of property in the two areas were then compared to determine the independent effect of the pollution. Table 7-8 shows the estimated indices for 1957-1964. Also included is the probability that the observed difference between the index values for the affected and control areas for a given year is due to sampling error (two-tailed test). The null hypothesis is that the true difference is zero.

If the two areas are comparable the indices for the affected and control areas should not be significantly different prior to 1962 so that significant divergences after 1962 could be expected to reflect the effects of pollution. Except for 1959 and 1960, there is no significant difference between indices at the 10 percent level of significance. In 1959 and 1960 the probability that the large difference was due to sampling error was only 2 percent and 10 percent, respectively. No evidence was found to explain this unexpected divergence in the indices for these years.

Table 7-8
Regression Index: Property Values, 1957-1964

Year	Regression Index Affected Area	Regression Index Control Area	P^a	Number of Sales Affected Area	Number of Sales Control Area
1957	100.0	100.0	–	47	96
1958	98.6	97.7	.60	30	76
1959	97.9	112.0	.02	37	96
1960	103.6	114.0	.10	34	71
1961	99.0	108.4	.40	19	64
1962	100.3	102.0	.60	30	62
1963	94.2	101.6	.10	34	68
1964[b]	90.8	103.8	.06	10	20

[a]P is the probability that the observed difference between the index values for the affected and control areas for a given year is due to sampling error (two-tailed test). The null hypothesis under test here is that the true difference is zero.

[b]First six months only.

The likelihood that sampling error could have resulted in such a large divergence in the indices in 1963 and 1964 is only 10 percent and 6 percent.[b] Thus, there is evidence that property values diverged significantly after pollution began in 1962. Nevertheless, if one uses a 5 percent level of significance, there is no statistically significant difference in the indices after pollution!

If we were discussing a house that was $10,000 in 1957, which is slightly less than the median value of single-family houses in tract 15C (includes more than the affected area) in 1960 ($12,000), the house in the affected area would have declined $583 in 1963 and a total of $1,023 by 1964, while the house in the control area would have declined only $40 in 1963 and returned to a level of $180 above the 1962 level by 1964. For the one-and-one-half year period the decline of property value in the affected area may have been as much as $1,000. A rough estimate of the total loss in the neighborhood, based on the number of dwelling units in the affected area, is $765,000.

For a number of reasons this estimate must be interpreted with caution. First, while $1,000 for each house and $765,000 for all houses in the affected area is the best estimate of the loss attributable to the increased level of air pollution, it is subject to a relatively wide margin of error. Similar differences between the affected and control areas occurred in 1959 and 1960 for no apparent reason. This same unknown factor may have operated again in 1963 and 1964. Furthermore, one and one-half years after pollution may be too short a time period.

[b]Except for its unfortunate effect upon sample size, no particular significance can be attached to the fact that data are available only for the first half of 1964. It is doubtful that a seasonal pattern exists; but if it does, it is almost certainly the same for both areas studied.

Second, it was impossible to control for the effects of expectations about the permanence of the higher level of pollution. Property values could be expected to drop by more if both buyers and sellers believed that the higher level of air pollution was going to be permanent than if they believed it was likely to be temporary. Since local residents were successful in forcing the factory to install pollution control equipment—and when that proved to be unsatisfactory to suspend operations for a time—it is plausible that they believed the pollution would be temporary. Thus, our estimate of the loss due to pollution may be low.

There is no evidence whether the relative income level of the neighborhood changed because of the pollution. Therefore, we do not know whether there is an income effect in the $1,000 decline.

Conclusion

We have two estimates of the impact of air pollution on property values in the St. Louis Metropolitan Area. On the one hand we have an estimate of a decrease of $245 for every increase of 0.5 milligrams in the level of sulfur trioxide per 100 square centimeters per day. On the other hand, we have an estimate of a decrease of $1,000 in house values caused by a specific nuisance. They are difficult to compare because of the different circumstances for each. Nevertheless, both fit into the theoretical structure of the housing market as set forth in this paper. They are the first attempts that I know about for estimating the actual magnitude of air pollution on property values.

There will never be a single estimate of the effect of air pollution on house values. In every case the actual impact of pollution will depend on the total array of houses available in a particular city, as well as the income distribution and tastes of the households allocated among the houses. It is therefore apparent that it is illegitimate to use the impact of pollution on house values in one place as a measure of its impact in another. One cannot use these estimates to indicate the impact of pollution on values in Los Angeles.

Notes

1. Alfred Marshall, PRINCIPLES OF ECONOMICS (8th edition, New York, New York: Macmillan Company, 1920), pp. 803-804.

2. Richard M. Hurd, PRINCIPLES OF CITY LAND VALUES (New York, New York: Record and Guide, 1924), pp. 77-78.

3. Richard U. Ratcliff, URBAN LAND ECONOMICS (New York, New York: McGraw Hill Book Company, 1949), p. 114.

4. Walter R. Kuehle, THE APPRAISAL OF REAL ESTATE (Chicago, Illinois: R.R. Donnelly and Sons Company, 1964), pp. 92-93.

5. For the detailed study see Ronald Ridker, editor, ECONOMIC COSTS OF AIR POLLUTION (New York, New York: Frederick Praeger Press, 1967).

6. See Richard F. Muth, "Economic Change and Rural-Urban Land Conversions," ECONOMETRICA (January 1961), pp. 1-23; William Alonso, LOCATION AND LAND USE (Cambridge, Massachusetts: Harvard University Press, 1964); and Lowdon Wingo, TRANSPORTATION AND URBAN LAND (Washington, D.C.: Resources for the Future, 1961).

7. Bureau of the Census, UNITED STATES CENSUS OF POPULATION AND HOUSING: 1960, CENSUS TRACTS, Final Report PHC (1)-131 (Washington, D.C.: Government Printing Office, 1962), p. 139.

8. Richard F. Muth, "The Spatial Structure of the Housing Market," PAPER AND PROCEEDINGS OF THE REGIONAL SCIENCE ASSOCIATION, 1961, pp. 207-220; and Edgar M. Hoover and Raymond Vernon, ANATOMY OF A METROPOLIS (Garden City, New York: Doubleday and Company, 1962), pp. 135-145.

9. Hoover and Vernon, ibid., p. 153.

10. Ibid., pp. 146-174.

11. FILTERING AND NEIGHBORHOOD CHANGE, Research Report 24 of the Center for Real Estate and Urban Economics of the Institute of Urban and Regional Development at the University of California, Berkeley, 1964, pp. 17-33. For a formulation of the theory as an assignment problem in linear programming see, Wallace F. Smith, "The Housing Stock as a Resource," PAPERS AND PROCEEDINGS OF THE FIRST FAR EAST CONFERENCE OF THE REGIONAL SCIENCE ASSOCIATION, pp. 77-92.

12. R. Ridker, op. cit.

13. For details see ibid.

14. Petition to the City of St. Louis and State of Missouri to enforce existing laws on behalf of 270 residents, on file in the office of R.T. Dreher, attorney, St. Louis, Missouri.

8 The Effect of a Negative Income Tax on the Number of Substandard Housing Units

A negative income tax has been proposed by a number of economists and sociologists in recent years to help alleviate poverty. Support for some form of income supplement has come from a wide spectrum of political positions.[1] Milton Friedman in particular has suggested a 50 percent negative income tax as a substitute for current welfare programs.[2] His argument is that the poor would be better off with a lump sum of money than with particular benefits, such as public housing, because they could choose to spend the funds in any way that they wished.

Although there have been many studies on the impact of a negative income tax on work incentives and the federal treasury, no one has attempted to determine if such a policy would substitute for current housing policies which attempt to improve housing to some standard level.[3] Regardless of the motivation behind a negative income tax proposal, if it should have an impact on the quality of housing it would be useful to know what this impact would be in order to plan other housing legislation better.

An immediate difficulty in such a study is the definition of standard housing. On the one hand, a criterion based on market efficiency would be that standard housing is that quality that would cause the marginal social benefit (reduction of neighborhood cost of fire insurance, police protection, and welfare) to just equal

Source: Reprinted from LAND ECONOMICS, vol. 46, no. 4 (The University of Wisconsin Press, November 1970).

The author wishes to acknowledge an embarrassing amount of assistance. This study was financed in part by the Institute for Research on Poverty, the University of Wisconsin, for a summer research appointment and computer time. Partial funding was received through the summer studies program of the Center for Urban Studies at the University of Illinois, Chicago Circle Campus, financed by the Department of Housing and Urban Development. Certain data used in this report were derived from a computer tape furnished under a joint project sponsored by the United States Bureau of the Census and the Population Council and containing selected 1960 Census information for a 0.1 percent sample of the population of the United States. Neither the Census Bureau nor the Population Council assumes any responsibility for the validity of any of the figures or interpretations of the figures herein based on this material. Harold Watts, Burton Weisbrod, Larry Orr, Eugene Smolensky, other members of the staff of the Institute for Research on Poverty, and Richard F. Muth have made useful comments. In addition I have benefitted from discussions with Jane Leuthold, Ralph Husby, Harold F. Williamson, Jr., and Julian Simon, all members of the Department of Economics, the University of Illinois. Between the preliminary version of this study and its final draft William G. Grigsby allowed me to have a copy of a preliminary paper of his on this same subject. I have benefitted from his careful analysis of the complexities of the relation between a guaranteed income plan and the housing market. (See Note 3.) Needless to say, I alone am responsible for remaining errors of commission and omission.

the marginal cost of improving quality an additional degree, whatever that might be. On the other hand, a criterion might be that standard housing is that quality of housing that society believes to be minimal for decent living. Either criterion is nearly impossible to implement empirically. We will use the definition used by many housing analysts and which relies mostly on the latter criterion. It is in negative form, defining substandard instead of standard housing. Substandard housing will be defined as a unit that lacks some or all plumbing facilities, or is dilapidated. Dilapidation is the presence of defects making a structure unsafe.

This study is an attempt to estimate the effect of one specific negative income tax plan on the number of substandard housing units, as defined above, in the United States. An operational model showing how a change in income distribution might affect the quality of housing is presented first. It is followed by empirical estimation of the impact of a 50 percent negative income tax on the housing market of 1960. Specifically, we will use the 50 percent Friedman plan. That is, when a family's income falls below its tax deductions and exemptions, they will receive a benefit equal to 50 percent of the difference between their allowable deductions and exemptions and their income. Under the current tax law the allowable deductions and exemptions are as follows: A basic $200 deduction for each family plus $100 for each person in the family and the standard $600 exemption for each member of the family. Thus, the allowable deductions and exemptions for a single person would be $900 and for a family of four would be $3,000.

The Model

In this study we want to determine whether a given improvement in housing units will occur. In the real estate market, investors often make this kind of decision. They have to estimate whether to build a particular kind of property in one place or another, or whether to improve a property and, if so, by how much. Their investment decision depends on whether the present value of incomes from the property will support the costs of construction. The problem is identical to the one undertaken in this study, so that we shall also use this approach.[4]

The present value of annual net income from real property can be expressed in the following way:

$$V = \sum_{n=1}^{N} \frac{a}{(1+r)^n} = \left[\frac{(1+r)^n - 1}{r(1+r)^n} \right] a \qquad a = Ba \tag{1}$$

where V =   present value of income from property[a]

        a =   expected gross annual income and is also equal to the rent expenditure of the tenant

        N =   the economic life of the structure, or the period of time during which the investor wants to recapture his investment

        r =   the sum of the tax rate, rate for maintenance and repair, a vacancy rate, and the opportunity cost of capital

        n =   years 1 through N

$$B = \frac{(1+r)^n - 1}{r(1+r)^n} = \text{gross rent multiplier}[5]$$

At any time an investor will convert, merge, or improve real property, if the cost is equal to or less than the increase in value caused by the change. An improvement will occur if

$$C \leqslant V' - V \qquad (2)$$

where V' =   the present value after change

        V =   the present value if there should be no change

        C =   the cost of conversion, merger, or improvement

The rule applies to conversion of land from agricultural to urban land use, as well as the conversion of single family houses to rooming houses, the demolition of old houses to construct an office building, or the improvement in quality of a residential building. In each circumstance the investor must estimate the expected annual income from the property before and after change, the expected life of the investment before and after change, and the opportunity cost of his capital.

Knowing this information an alternative way to represent the decision equation can be constructed in the following way:

$$C = B'c' - Ba \qquad (3)$$

---

[a]Actually there should be no depreciation of land, so that the present value of land (V_1) would be calculated as follows:

$$V_1 = \frac{a}{r}$$

where a = annual net income to land and r = the opportunity cost of capital.

Appraisers of a real property investment would calculate the land value separate from building value, compute the return necessary for land, and deduct this from the net annual income of the property. Equation (1) would then be used to calculate the present value of the building. Nevertheless, any separation of land and building value is arbitrary and fictitious. For source see note 4.

where B' = the gross rent multiplier after change
c' = the gross annual rent after change necessary to make $V' - V$ equal cost
B = the gross rent multiplier before change
a = the gross annual rent expected before change

If the gross rent multiplier (B') after change would be equal to the multiplier (B), then Equation (3) becomes

$$C = B(c' - a) \tag{4}$$

and the expected change in value would be

$$V' - V = B(a' - a) \tag{5}$$

where a' = the expected gross annual rent after change. Thus, an improvement, conversion, or other change would be undertaken so long as

$$C \leqslant V' - V \tag{2}$$

Substituting Equations (4) and (5) into (2),

$$B(c' - a) \leqslant B(a' - a)$$

Dividing through by B, we obtain

$$c' - a \leqslant a' - a$$

or

$$\frac{c' - a}{a} \leqslant \frac{a' - a}{a} \tag{6}$$

This inequality shows that under the above assumption that $B' = B$, an investor will undertake a given change so long as the percentage increase in rent required to make the change in value equal to cost is equal to or less than the expected percentage increase in rents. The assumption that gross rent multipliers are equal before and after a change in use would be inappropriate for most types of changes in real property because the multiplier is a function of the economic life of the structure, the tax rate, rate for maintenance and repair, vacancy rate, and the opportunity cost of capital. Nevertheless, the equality of the multipliers may be a reasonable approximation for the rehabilitation of substandard housing.

We now need to determine how the gross annual rent, a, of any property is established. The gross annual rents, hereafter called the rents, are established in local housing markets. The operation of these local housing markets can be shown to be similar to an assignment problem.[6] Consider a given community with a finite number of housing units of varying quality. There are as many families seeking housing as there are units. Each family is willing to bid a particular rent for each of the available housing units. The rent bid depends upon family preferences, incomes, the quality of housing, and the location of the units. In particular, location includes the distance of the dwelling from jobs and shopping, its access to recreational facilities and distance from nuisance effects (such as air pollution and who is living in adjacent sites). If the families were already housed, these bids would represent bids on other houses and reservation bids on the one that they occupied. The latter, of course, must take account of the cost of moving to a new dwelling.

If there is competition in the property market, assignments of families to housing units will be such that rents will be maximized. Each family will occupy that house that it prefers the most and for which it can offer more rent than others. The rents established in this way are short-run equilibrium rents. There are two problems with this solution: first is that it is a short-run rather than long-run equilibrium; and second is that equilibrium rents do not exist if the above assumption that rents depend upon who occupies adjacent housing holds.

Let us take up the last problem first. Koopmans and Beckmann have shown that if each household rent bid is dependent upon who occupies the adjacent site, there is no set of rents that will cause an equilibrium.[7] There will always be at least one household that will find itself better off by moving to a new location. Such a result makes it awkward to apply comparative statics analysis because there is no settled equilibrium in the competitive housing market from which to analyze the impact of change. Therefore, in the analysis that follows we shall assume that each family's rent bid is independent of those families on adjacent sites.

Now we take up the first problem, which was that the assignment solution to the market is a short-run equilibrium. We shall try to adapt the short-run model to long-run equilibrium by introducing rehabilitation and repair into the analysis. Perhaps some families after their assignments would be willing to pay increases in rents in order to improve the quality of the units that they occupy. Whether such quality improvements occur depends upon costs and the families' willingness and ability to pay, as indicated by Inequality (6). If the percentage increase in rent families would pay is greater than the percentage increase in rent necessary to pay off the cost, then the improvements would occur. If the improvements would be sufficient to make the housing unit competitive with previously better housing, the supply of such housing would increase, and the rents on that quality would have a tendency to fall. These rents would continue to fall until they were equal to the rent necessary to pay off the cost of improvements. After all such improvements have been completed the long-run equilibrium for a stable population would be achieved.

Consider a change in the distribution of income among the families, such as would occur with a negative income tax. The above long-run equilibrium would be disturbed. Some families would find their incomes reduced by the increased taxes necessary to finance the negative income tax. Other families would find their incomes increased because their earnings were below their allowable deductions and exemptions. Since rent bids are a function of income, some rent bids will rise and others will fall. Furthermore, since there are many more families who will be taxed than there are families for whom benefits will be allowed, individual decreases in incomes and rents will be much smaller than increases. We shall consider these decreases to be negligible and we shall therefore ignore them.

Because of the redistribution of income there would be a new array of rent bids for each of the existing housing units. At the upper end of the distribution there would be no change in rank order of bids, although each bid might be somewhat less. At the lower end, however, there would be a new income floor below which families do not fall. The income floor is different for different size families, being higher for families with more persons. Since the benefits vary by family size and income, some families might be able to move up in the rank order by income. Therefore, there might be some initial shifting of families into different quality units. In particular families with more persons may be able to shift up at the expense of smaller families. Since the average income of families receiving benefits has risen, all bids of these families would tend to rise. Nevertheless, with higher incomes, higher bids can also be made for improvements in quality. Thus, after the initial rise in bids there would be the secondary effect of families that would pay more to have their assigned unit improved. In some cases their bid would be sufficient to improve quality. Improvements would continue to occur until the increase in rents was forced down to equality with the cost of improving houses to better quality.

To work out the empirical problem we need to make several assumptions with respect to the above model. They will cause our results to be only approximations, and to the extent that these assumptions are unacceptable to others, the results will be questioned. Since there is no possibility at this time of estimating the accuracy of the predictions, we must look to the reasonableness of the assumptions.

As noted above, the first assumption that is necessary is that a family's demand for housing is independent of the decisions of other families. Obviously this assumption is not true. Indeed, the interdependence of consumer preferences for housing has been considered as one of the factors preventing rehabilitation of neighborhoods, when such rehabilitation would otherwise be profitable.[8] If one house in a blighted neighborhood were to be improved, its rent would not rise much and might not rise sufficiently to pay the cost of the improvement. The rent is held down by the general quality of property in the neighborhood. In such a situation the private market may be unable to improve blighted neighborhoods, even if it should be profitable to do so. It is important to recognize, however, that such neighborhoods may not generate sufficiently high rents for improvement, even if the interdependency of consumer demand were not present. There are at least three reasons for accepting the reasonableness of the assumption that consumer demands are independent for our analysis. First, a negative income tax plan would cause a general shift in demand in the same neighborhood, so there might be pressure for a general improvement of a neighborhood. Second, there is an allowable amount of variation among rents in the same neighborhood even when preferences are interdependent. Third, so long as there are vacancies in the stock of housing, competition to hold families with negative income tax benefits would result in improved housing. Families with income supplements might be able to pay the higher rents for vacant standard housing. If substandard housing vacancies rose as a result, their owners would be forced to improve them or lose all revenue.

The second assumption is that the income elasticity of demand for housing is unity. The percentage increase in rent that families would be willing and able to pay would be equal to the percentage increase in their income. Recent studies of the income elasticity of demand for housing in the United States and other countries show a range between 0.3 and 2 or 3.[9] Most estimates are in the range of 0.6 to 1.

The third assumption is that there will be no change in the costs of home repairs and improvements because of any increase in construction activity caused by the negative income tax benefits. There have been no studies of the supply elasticity of the residential construction industry that I have been able to find. There are, however, several facts indicating that the industry is a constant cost industry. One study found that the expansion and contraction of the industry was swift during periods of change and showed little change in costs per dwelling unit.[10] Although a massive increase in home improvements could cause increases in such costs in order to bid resources away from alternative employments, the shift may cause the industry to reorganize and find more efficient ways of doing operations currently performed on a custom basis. Greater efficiency might result in home improvement costs decreasing in the long run. Since there seems to be no clear-cut evidence for either decreasing or increasing costs, the assumption that no change in costs will occur is made.

The investment model together with the last three assumptions allows estimation of the effect of the negative income tax on the number of substandard housing units improved to standard quality. For each substandard housing unit, one needs to estimate the percentage increase in rent necessary to support the rehabilitation of that house to standard quality, $(c' - a)/a$; and the percentage increase in rent that families would pay out of increases in income from negative income tax benefits $(a' - a)/a$. Applying Inequality (6), the total number of housing units for which the latter exceeds the former is a measure of the impact of a negative income tax.

Such a census would be exceedingly costly. An alternative is to randomly select a number of families, pay them the benefits that they would receive from a negative income tax plan, see how they spend their increase on rent, and count how many of their housing units are improved to standard quality. An experimental study along these lines on many aspects of a negative income tax is being tried for a three-year period.[11] The main difficulty in using this study for an analysis of housing is its short time horizon. Many home improvements will require longer than three years to be paid off through increased rents.

In this study, probability distributions of the percentage increase in rent families would pay for improved housing with income supplements and of the percentage increase in rents required to improve substandard housing units to standard quality will be estimated from two separate data sources. On the basis that they are independent events, these two distributions will be combined into a joint probability distribution from which one can estimate the proportion of substandard units that will be upgraded to standard quality.

Empirical Analysis

The probability distribution of the percentage increase in rent that families would pay for improved housing was estimated by applying a 50 percent negative income tax to a selected group of families in the 0.1 percent sample of the 1960 Census. Because of the limitations of the data, the analysis was restricted to primary families or individuals who occupied substandard non-farm housing units by paying rent for a unit in any structure, or by right of ownership of a single-family unit detached from other housing units or from a business establishment. The study group was further restricted to the above families and individuals whose head earned income solely from wages and salaries or self-employment.[b]

The study group was restricted to non-farm housing because the cost data were generated from an urban blighted area. Costs in that area may not be representative of rural farm rehabilitation costs. Of course, the same logic may apply to the use of the cost information for rural non-farm housing, but we will take the chance.

Total family income reported by the Census includes a third category besides wages and salaries and self-employment income. This third category includes welfare payments, pensions, social security payments, patent payments, and royalties and rents. We would have liked to exclude only families currently

---

[b]There were 3,282 families in the study group as defined in the text: 1,136 were in owner-occupied units and 2,146 were in tenant-occupied units. Multiplication by 1,000 yields the size of the universe in 1960 from which the families were sampled.

receiving welfare payments but that was impossible with the data. Instead we excluded all families whose head earned any income from the third category mentioned above. Because families may include several sub-families and other earners, members other than the head may be on welfare, but it seems unlikely since receipt of welfare payments depends on evidence of need. To the extent that poor families in substandard housing earn income wholly or partly from some source other than wages and salaries or self-employment the study group will yield an underestimate of the number of families receiving benefits.

There were three reasons for the basic selection of the study group. The first was that if families receiving welfare payments had not been excluded, the study would add negative income tax benefits on top of current welfare benefits. This would surely inflate the benefits that would be received under any negative income tax program. The second was that occupants of substandard housing now receiving welfare have not moved from substandard to standard housing. The supplements proposed in the income guarantee plans fall below the assistance payments now made to families with dependent children in two-fifths to two-thirds of the states.[12] Thus, if these families received a negative income tax benefit instead of their current benefits they would certainly not move into standard quality housing. The third follows from the second. If current welfare payments are higher than a negative income tax benefit, they could be meeting needs that a negative income tax plan would not, so that any negative income tax plan that is implemented will likely assist families not covered by the current welfare policies rather than substitute for current welfare programs.[13]

There is one final problem that needs to be covered before presenting the data. The families and individuals defined by the Census may not be the same group as the unit filing an income tax return. For example, married children may live with one set of parents and file separate income tax returns so that they would be separate families for income tax purposes. In the Census, however, they would be counted as one family living in the same housing unit. Total income reported is that for both families and not just for the head of the household. Therefore, this study will probably underestimate the benefits received. Some families living with relatives might find it possible to set up separate housekeeping if a negative income tax program were instituted. This reinforces the underestimation caused by excluding families whose income is low and is earned from sources other than wages and salaries, or self-employment.

Estimates of the benefits to the study group from a 50 percent negative income tax can be expressed as a relative frequency distribution of the percentage increase in income. These estimates were calculated from data grouped by income class and family size. For the most part the families were grouped by $250 income classes and exact family size so that the estimates are fairly refined. Because of our assumption that the income elasticity of demand for housing is equal to unity, this relative frequency distribution also shows the distribution of families by the percentage increase in rent that they would pay should they receive benefits under a 50 percent negative income tax plan. The distributions for owner- and tenant-occupied units are shown in the last row of Tables 8-1 and 8-2.

An estimate of the probability distribution of the percentage increase in rent that would be required to cover the cost of rehabilitating housing to standard quality was taken directly from a study by Schaaf in which these calculations were made for a slum area in Oakland, California.[14] A 25 percent simple random sample of residential properties in Census Tract 17 in Oakland were appraised for quality using the American Public Health Association (APHA) point system. A subsample of 56 properties was inspected by an architect and by a contractor. They made an estimate of the cost of upgrading each property to a specified standard, a standard similar to that used in this study. The standard was defined as follows:

In effect the standard requires the provision of private bath, toilet and kitchen facilities for each dwelling unit plus remedying of any imminently dangerous conditions for which the code (Oakland) reference is clear and unambiguous. It is assumed that the work would represent the absolute minimum needed and would generally be done in a spirit of unwilling compliance. The emphasis would be upon the avoidance of prosecution rather than upon the possibility that the work done might increase the value of the property.[15]

These code compliance cost estimates for the subsample were projected by Schaaf to the whole sample by means of regression equations estimated from the subsample relating the code compliance cost per room to APHA points. From market data on interest rates, economic life, taxes, and maintenance expenditures, gross rent multipliers were estimated. Then, using Equation (3) above, estimates of the increase in rent necessary to pay off the code compliance cost were made. Converting these estimates to percentages of current rent, Schaaf obtained the distribution of percentage increases in rent required to pay off the rehabilitation costs shown in the last column of Tables 8-1 and 8-2.[c]

Since the distribution of rents families would pay has come from a different study than that of rents required to pay off rehabilitation, and since the Schaaf study did not indicate the association between family income, family size, and cost of code compliance, there is no direct evidence about the association between the percentage increase in rents families would pay and the percentage increase in rents necessary to pay off the rehabilitation cost. In the absence of such evidence we shall assume that these two events are independent random events. The relative frequency distribution for each event represents its probability distribution. By making this assumption the joint probability of any pair of possible increases in rents families would pay and required rent increases can be

[c]There were 655 renter units and 41 owner units for which cost estimates were made. Some did not require any rehabilitation. These were dropped so the distributions in Tables 8-1 and 8-2 are based on 634 renter units and 35 owner units.

Table 8-1
Tenant-Occupied Units in Study, Relative Frequency Distribution

Percentage Increase in Rents Required to Improve Housing[b]	Percentage Increase in Rents Families Would Pay[a]												
	0	1-10	11-20	21-30	31-40	41-60	61-80	81-100	101-120	121-140	141-160	over 160	Total
0	0	0	0	0	0	0	0	0	0	0	0	0	0
1- 10	.085	.011	.004	.007	.003	.006	.004	.003	.002	.001	0	.015	.142
11- 20	.057	.007	.008	.005	.002	.004	.003	.002	.001	.001	0	.010	.095
21- 30	.043	.005	.002	.004	.002	.003	.002	.001	.001	.001	0	.008	.072
31- 40	.043	.005	.002	.004	.001	.003	.002	.001	.002	.001	0	.008	.071
41- 60	.077	.010	.004	.007	.003	.005	.004	.002	.002	.001	0	.014	.129
61- 80	.065	.008	.003	.006	.002	.005	.003	.002	.002	.001	0	.012	.109
81-100	.060	.007	.003	.005	.002	.004	.003	.002	.002	.001	0	.011	.101
101-120	.047	.006	.002	.004	.002	.003	.003	.002	.001	.001	0	.008	.079
121-140	.059	.007	.003	.005	.001	.004	.003	.001	.001	.001	0	.011	.099
141-160	.031	.004	.002	.003	.001	.002	.002	.001	.001	.001	0	.006	.052
over 160	.030	.004	.002	.003	.001	.002	.001	.001	.001	.001	.003	.005	.050
TOTAL	.599	.074	.031	.051	.021	.042	.029	.018	.014	.010	.003	.107	1.00

[a]Equals percent increase in income resulting from 50% negative income tax as a result of assuming income elasticity is one. Calculated from 0.1 percent sample from 1960 Census.

[b]Recalculated from A.H. Schaaf, ECONOMIC ASPECTS OF URBAN RENEWAL: THEORY, POLICY AND AREA ANALYSIS, Research Report Number 14, Real Estate Research Program, Institute of Business and Economic Research, University of California, Berkeley, 1960, pp. 34, 37, by dropping units requiring no rehabilitation costs.

Table 8-2
Owner-Occupied Single Family Units in Study, Relative Frequency Distribution

Percentage Increase in Rents Required to Improve Housing[b]	Percentage Increase in Rents Families Would Pay[a]								Total
	0	1-10	11-20	21-30	31-40	41-50	51-100	over 100	
0	0	0	0	0	0	0	0	0	0
1- 10	.106	.017	.007	.013	.005	.005	.013	.033	.200
11- 20	.106	.017	.007	.013	.005	.005	.013	.033	.200
21- 30	.076	.012	.005	.010	.004	.004	.010	.024	.143
31- 40	.076	.012	.005	.010	.004	.004	.010	.024	.143
41- 50	.046	.007	.003	.006	.002	.002	.006	.014	.086
51-100	.091	.014	.006	.011	.004	.004	.011	.029	.171
over 100	.030	.005	.002	.004	.001	.001	.004	.010	.057
TOTAL	.530	.085	.033	.067	.026	.026	.067	.167	1.00

[a]Same as Table 8-1.

[b]Same as Table 8-1.

calculated. It is simply the product of (1) the probability that any family in substandard housing without welfare payments will receive a given percentage increase in income from negative income tax benefits (or the same thing, will be willing and able to increase rent a given percentage) and (2) the probability of a substandard housing unit requiring a given percentage increase in rent to pay off the rehabilitation cost. These probabilities are shown in Tables 8-1 and 8-2.

All those families for whom the percentage increase in rent they would pay is greater than the percentage increase in rent that would be required to pay off rehabilitation costs would be able to improve their substandard housing unit to standard quality. The step lines through Tables 8-1 and 8-2 divide the cells into those groups that can improve their housing to standard quality and those that cannot. All of those cells above the line are groups for whom the rent increase they could pay is greater than that required to rehabilitate. For those cells below the line the rent increase required for rehabilitation is greater. Summing over all the cells above the line, the probability that a tenant living in substandard housing and who receives income only from wages and salaries or self-employment will rehabilitate his house to standard quality is 0.24. That is, 24 percent of such families will be likely to rehabilitate their housing to standard quality. In the same way, 43 percent of those families living in their own substandard detached housing unit and receiving income only from wages and salaries or self-employment would rehabilitate their house to standard quality.

Applying these percentages to the appropriate estimates of the total number of families in owner- and tenant-occupied substandard non-farm housing units and earning wage and salary income or self-employed income, we find that the total number of units that would have been improved to standard quality in 1960 would have been about 857,000 units. If the income elasticity of demand for housing should be only 0.5 rather than the one that was assumed, this estimate of the reduction of substandard housing would be reduced to about 465,000 units. As a point of comparison, 850,228 public housing units have been constructed in almost thirty years.[16] Nevertheless, there were about 11 million substandard housing units in the United States in 1960.[17]

Conclusion

The magnitude of our estimate of the number of housing units that would be improved to standard quality because of benefits received from a 50 percent negative income tax suggests that a guaranteed income policy could be as important an influence on the quality of housing as current public housing policy. Its impact is great enough that it is worth further study.

The model described in the first part of the paper outlines the considerations necessary for analyzing the problem of the impact of a change in income distribution on the quality of housing. In empirically implementing the model, however, several assumptions were required. In particular, it was assumed that the income elasticity of demand for housing is unity, and that the home repair and improvement industry is a constant cost industry. The first assumption can be defended by a number of statistical studies. The second assumption cannot be defended by reference to statistical tests. The tests do not exist.

The estimates of the percentage increases in rent required to rehabilitate substandard housing are weak. Further study is required into the supply side of the housing market. We know very little about the nature of rehabilitation costs. Although there have been many demonstration projects, the data from these studies have not been analyzed in such a way as to be useful for understanding the supply of improvements. There is also a noticeable lack of information on the housing of welfare recipients. For the purposes of this study it would be useful to know how the quality of their housing changed, or if it did at all, as a result of welfare benefits received.

The model presented was not constructed for the sake of building a model, but to help understand the impact of a negative income tax on the number of substandard housing units. The model itself is useful because it outlines the major facts needed in any such analysis. The empirical implementation has shown that such a policy may have as important an impact as current housing policy. But more importantly, the attempt at implementation has indicated the kind of further research required to do a better analysis.

Notes

1. For a general survey of these proposals and the reasons for their support see, Clair Wilcox, TOWARD SOCIAL WELFARE (Homewood, Illinois: Richard D. Irwin, Incorporated, 1969), pp. 248-269.

2. Milton Friedman, CAPITALISM AND FREEDOM (Chicago, The University of Chicago Press, 1962), especially pp. 190-195.

3. For a recent bibliography see, Gail Schlachter, "Guaranteed Annual Income: A Selected Bibliography of Current Materials" (Unpublished paper, Institute for Research on Poverty, University of Wisconsin, 1967). Since beginning my own research, I have learned of another similar study on the impact of guaranteed annual income on housing markets: William G. Grisby, "Possible Impacts of the Guaranteed Annual Income on Housing Markets" (Unpublished paper, March 1969).

4. Ralph Turvey, ECONOMICS OF REAL PROPERTY (London, George Allen and Unwin, 1957), pp. 8-24.

5. For a proof that this is the multiplier necessary to make a constant annual sum equal to its present value see John G. Kemeny et al. FINITE MATHEMATICS WITH BUSINESS APPLICATIONS (Englewood Cliffs, New Jersey: Prentice-Hall, Inc., 1962), pp. 312-320.

6. Martin Beckmann, LOCATION THEORY (New York, Random House, 1968) pp. 94-96; also, Wallace F. Smith, "The Housing Stock as a Resource," PAPERS AND PROCEEDINGS OF THE FIRST FAR EAST CONFERENCE OF THE REGIONAL SCIENCE ASSOCIATION, 1965, pp. 77-92.

7. Tjalling Koopmans and Martin Beckmann, "Assignment Problems and the Location of Economic Activities," ECONOMETRICA (1957), pp. 53-76; also, Beckmann, loc. cit.

8. Otto A. Davis and Andrew B. Whinston, "The Economics of Urban Renewal," LAW AND CONTEMPORARY PROBLEMS (Winter 1961), pp. 100-110.

9. Margaret Reid, HOUSING AND INCOME (Chicago, Illinois: The University of Chicago Press, 1962); Tong Hun Lee, "Housing and Permanent Income: Tests Based on a Three Year Reinterview Survey," REVIEW OF ECONOMICS AND STATISTICS (November 1968), pp. 480-490; also, Hendrik S. Houthakker, "An International Comparison of Household Expenditure Patterns, Commemorating the Centenary of Engel's Law," ECONOMETRICA (October 1957), pp. 532-51.

10. Sherman J. Maisel, HOUSEBUILDING IN TRANSITION (Berkeley, University of California, 1953).

11. Harold W. Watts, "Graduated Work Incentives: An Experiment in Negative Taxation," AMERICAN ECONOMIC REVIEW (May 1969), pp. 463-472.

12. Wilcox, op. cit., p. 258.

13. Ibid., p. 257-259.

14. A.H. Schaaf, ECONOMIC ANALYSIS OF URBAN RENEWAL: THEORY, POLICY AND AREA ANALYSIS, Research Report Number 14, Real Estate Research Program, Institute of Business and Economic Research, University of California, Berkeley, 1960.

89

15. Ibid., p. 20.

16. United States Bureau of the Census, STATISTICAL ABSTRACT OF THE UNITED STATES: 1968 (89th edition) Washington, D.C., 1968, p. 706.

17. Ibid.

The Filtering Process: The Webster Groves and Kankakee Cases *

(With Donald Guy)

Introduction

The filtering concept has had a long history in the analysis of appropriate public policy toward housing the poor. There are many definitions, but most would fit the following description. Owners of good quality housing buy new housing in order to avoid technological or economic obsolescence. The values of older housing then fall, and families with lower incomes can afford to buy and improve the quality of their housing. Thus, in order to conserve on housing stock, one efficient policy is to build new housing of the best quality, allow the filtering process to function, and leave only the poorest housing stock empty and ready for demolition.

Anthony Downs has pointed out that this has indeed been the implicit, if not explicit, housing policy carried out by the United States.[1] In spite of public housing construction, most subsidies have been to middle- and upper-income families; this has been accompanied by enforcement of high or moderate standards for all new construction.

Although filtering has been discussed in journals and books, and although government policy has been based on the theory, few empirical studies have been made to test the hypothesis. It is true that Hoyt's original hypothesis was based on empirical evidence from census studies of many cities.[2] Nevertheless, it was based on cross-sectional rather than on time-series analysis of particular neighborhoods and houses. Recently, Lansing, Clifton, and Morgan have made an analysis of the moves of families into new homes.[3] They traced the successive moves which were caused by families relinquishing an old house and moving into a new house. From their evidence, we do find that new housing construction sets off a sequence of moves that extends to poor families. But many questions remain unanswered. Is there a subsequent decline in maintenance? Do values decline relatively? The above study shows that the sequence of moves tends to move toward the center of the city. Are there any other characteristics about the neighborhood in which filtering takes place? Does filtering automatically follow aging?

These are questions that require a different set of data than the census data used by Hoyt, and the cross-section survey by Lansing, Clifton, and Morgan.

Reprinted from PAPERS AND PROCEEDINGS OF THE AMERICAN REAL ESTATE AND URBAN ECONOMICS ASSOCIATION, 5 (December 1970).

*The authors, from the University of Montana and the University of Missouri-St. Louis, respectively, were ably assisted by several research assistants who received financing in part from the Center for Community and Metropolitan Studies at the University of Missouri-St. Louis.

Purpose

This paper is an attempt to show how a different source of data might be used to study the question of filtering. Since around 1917 to 1926, city directories have been compiled on a regular basis every two years or more, often by the R.L. Polk Company. We would like to show how this data might be used to study the question of filtering in housing markets. The two areas studied, Webster Groves and Kankakee, were selected because of the availability of additional data which was unavailable in the city directory. Our approach will be to study the successive occupants of a selected group of houses. The reason for requiring additional sources of data was to see if interpretation of the Polk data could be made without other information, such as price, in other later studies, since regular relations might be found between filtering and price or other variables.

Data

Let's start with a description of the data source: The R.L. Polk City Directories. In these directories, all heads of households are listed alphabetically. The listing includes the person's address, occupation, and sometimes place of employment. There is a second listing of households by address. This second list is the sampling population that we have worked with. After selecting a year to begin the analysis, such as the first year for which directories are available in the particular place, the houses to be traced were chosen. The data collection then proceeded by recording who occupies each house in the study in each year or for selected years that the directory is available. This caught most changes in occupancy, but not all of them. In the two years between directories, two or three turnovers might have occurred, rather than the one that would be revealed by the directory.

There is no question that there are also errors in the directory. We have tried to clean up as many errors as possible. But those that we found were obvious errors from inconsistencies within the directory's two different lists of households.

Occupational information is also listed in the directory under the alphabetical listing of persons. These were converted to estimates of income rank by reference to census data showing the decile ranking for occupations. The underlying assumption of such a procedure was that income is a function of occupation. It would be desirable to know a person's actual income, but such data were not available. It is not strictly necessary to assume that all income is from wages and salaries, but it is sometimes necessary to assume that non-wage income is proportional to wage income. When using the census income rankings, the non-wage income is included in the annual income for each occupation; thus, this is obviously the best source. However, it is only available for 1939, 1949, and 1959.[4]

There is some dispersion of earnings within an occupational category, and in some occupations the range of earnings overlaps. The income proxy necessarily assumes that the worker is near the median earnings for his occupation. The possibility for error in the rankings increases, the more narrow the differential between occupations and the greater the dispersion of earnings within occupational categories.

Since the object of the income analysis was to determine rank order, it was not always necessary to know the income level of a given occupation but only its rank in relation to another occupation at that time. In many cases, it was not necessary to have occupational rankings for the exact year in which the filtering determination was made. If the relative rankings of two occupations were known to be the same for two points in time, it was assumed that they had the same rank between those dates. If the ranking changed, the rank for the nearest year was used. Various studies have shown that industry and occupational rankings change very slowly over time.[5]

Thus, our basic information is a time series of part of the sequence of persons living in a selected group of houses, along with the income rank of the occupations of those persons.

Operational Definition of Filtering

The criterion of whether or not filtering has occurred is based on a comparison of income levels for a succession of occupants. Consider the case of a house in which one occupant moves out and another occupant moves in. By definition, filtering down is said to occur if the income of the person moving out is higher than the income of the person moving into the same house. Filtering up, of course, would occur if the income of the person moving out is less than the income of the person moving into the same house.

There is still some difficulty with this definition. It is the same problem that occurs using the survey data of the Lansing, Clifton, and Morgan study. A person may move into a house with a low income at a young age. As his income increases with his own increase in skills and position, he may become dissatisfied with his own house and sell it for a new one. He sells it to another person whose income is equivalent to what his was at the time he originally purchased it. No one would argue that filtering has taken place under such circumstances. Although the definition suggested above does not account for this problem, we shall try some variations on the definition to see if the analysis is seriously affected.

By the definition of filtering given above, some houses would probably indicate filtering down and some would not. If a large sample of houses were taken, many of them should indicate that filtering down has taken place, if filtering down is a general phenomenon. If filtering is not a general phenomenon, few houses in the sample should give a positive test for filtering. If there were no systematic forces operating in the housing market, the occurrence of filtering by the definition given above would be a random process in which the probability of filtering down would equal that of filtering up. This dichotomy lends itself nicely to a statistical test of significance using a binomial distribution.[6] The statistical model may be set out as follows:

Let N = the number of houses in the sample in which a change of income has occurred through change in occupancy

x = the number of houses filtering down

y = the number of houses filtering up

Px = the probability that a house will filter down

Py = $1 - Px$ = the probability that a house will filter up

The null hypothesis is that $Px = Py = 0.5$. The alternative hypothesis is that $Px > Py$.

In each year, where year is defined arbitrarily as the year the new occupant is shown in the directory, sum the cases of filtering up and filtering down. The test as to whether filtering down in the neighborhood occurs is whether the actual numbers were likely to have occurred if the true probabilities were 0.5. The statistical test of significance is a one-tail test using a level of significance of 0.05.

Selection of Neighborhoods

The first areas studied were two small neighborhoods in Kankakee, Illinois. Kankakee was established by the Illinois Central Railroad and the Associates Land Company in 1853.[7] By 1855, it included 1,000 people. Except for the decades of 1900 to 1910 and 1950 to 1960, the rate of growth of population was greater than that for the United States.[8] The population in 1960 was 27,511. Two neighborhoods were selected from blocks in the original Associates Land Company plat of 1854 and the Associates First Addition, which was plated in 1855.

Neighborhood One is northeast of the central business district, while Neighborhood Two is southeast of the central business district.[a] The northern

---

[a]Neighborhood One has the following boundaries:
North—Big Four Railroad
East—North Rosewood Avenue
South—East Oak Street
West—North Harrison Avenue

Neighborhood Two has the following boundaries:
North—East Hickory Street
East—South Rosewood Avenue
South—Eagle Street
West—South Harrison Avenue

part of Neighborhood One borders the Big Four Railroad, which was completed in 1872, and the Big Four Depot. There are some commercial structures near the tracks, but the neighborhood is primarily residential. An unpublished study of employment status in Kankakee for the years 1896, 1925, and 1929-1930 shows that the area was 65 percent white collar in 1896.[9] By 1929, the area had become 51 percent blue collar.

Neighborhood Two is southeast of the central business district and about the same distance from it as is Neighborhood One. The study of employment status previously referred to shows that this neighborhood was 80 percent white collar in 1896, but had declined to 52 percent white collar by 1929-1930. This area was described, in a 1948 study by Harland Bartholomew and Associates, as an area of old homes which still had a desirable residential environment.[10]

Although they are in a small city, these two neighborhoods represent older neighborhoods adjacent to the central business district. Because of their age, they could be traced from 1916 to 1969. It was hoped that the selection of neighborhoods would enable us to determine neighborhood characteristics that might contribute to any filtering that might be found.

The second area, Webster Groves, Missouri, was selected in order to improve on the supplementary information that is available. There is a file of property values for the period 1917 to the present, to which one of the authors had access. The second reason for selection of Webster Groves was that, as a stable suburban community in the St. Louis metropolitan area, it could be used as a control group for comparisons of change across many districts in the entire metropolitan area. It is hoped that such comparisons will lead to more information on the factors causing neighborhood change and decline. Efforts are already underway to include two other suburbs in different sectors of the metropolitan area and which are equally distant from the St. Louis central business district.

Instead of selecting neighborhoods within Webster and running a time series on every house, a random sample of 138 addresses was taken, and the change in occupancy for each of these addresses from 1926 to 1969 was recorded.

In 1861, Webster was a station on the Missouri Pacific Railroad some ten miles from what is now downtown St. Louis.[11] In 1857, there were only three families living there. By 1911, there were over 7,000 people. Of these, 2,000 businessmen commuted by rail or trolley to St. Louis to work. By 1960, the population was 29,000 people, approximately the same size as Kankakee.[12] Although Webster grew as a dormitory suburb, with little or no industry, there were, however, many service workers living and working within the town. The sample was selected from blocks within the boundaries of Webster Groves in 1926. The boundaries were extended around 1936 through 1944.[13]

The Kankakee Case

The results obtained for the two neighborhoods in Kankakee are shown in Tables 9-1 and 9-2. One can see from Table 9-1 that three houses in Neighborhood One filtered up in 1918, while twelve houses filtered down in the same year. The probability of drawing a random sample with this distribution from a population in which the number of houses filtering down equalled the number of houses filtering up is 0.018. Thus, for that neighborhood for that year, the null hypothesis can be rejected at the 5 percent level of significance, and the alternative hypothesis can be accepted that filtering down occurred in the moves that took place in 1918. The null hypothesis is also rejected in 1929, 1931, and in 1954.

Filtering in Neighborhood Two is shown in Table 9-2. The null hypothesis was rejected for the years 1923, 1935, and 1959. Filtering up would have been statistically significant in 1925 if a two-tailed test had been selected. However, if

Table 9-1
Filtering by Income in Neighborhood One

Year	Filter Up By Income	Filter Down By Income	Probability[a]
1918	3	12	.018*
1923	6	6	.613
1925	7	13	.132
1927	11	12	.500
1929	5	15	.021*
1931	3	15	.004
1933	10	6	.454#
1935	16	8	.152#
1937	7	14	.095
1939	10	13	.339
1941	17	14	.720#
1949	10	9	.500
1954	7	24	.001*
1956	11	8	.648#
1958	8	8	.598
1959	10	7	.630#
1961	7	9	.402
1963	11	12	.500
1969	5	10	.151

[a]This column shows the probability of drawing a random sample from a population in which $P = Q = .5$ and finding a distribution equal to or more extreme than the one shown. Some probabilities are shown for a two-tailed test and are indicated by a # sign. Years in which the null hypothesis is rejected at the 5 per cent level are indicated by an *.

Table 9-2
Filtering by Income in Neighborhood Two

Year	Filter Up by Income	Filter Down by Income	Probability[a]
1918	6	5	0.500
1923	1	11	0.300*
1925	17	6	0.034#
1927	11	13	0.419
1929	4	8	0.194
1931	10	16	0.163
1933	10	15	0.212
1935	5	18	0.005*
1937	6	10	0.227
1939	12	10	0.832#
1941	18	11	0.264#
1949	9	15	0.154
1954	13	10	0.678#
1956	10	14	0.271
1958	9	12	0.332
1959	4	22	0.0002*
1961	4	5	0.500
1963	15	15	0.572
1969	8	13	0.192

[a]This column shows the probability of drawing a random sample from a population in which $P = Q = 0.5$ and finding a distribution equal to or more extreme than the one shown. Some probabilities are shown for a two-tailed test and are indicated by a # sign. Years in which the null hypothesis is rejected at the 5 per cent level are indicated by an *.

a two-tailed test had been used in all cases, filtering down would not have been statistically significant for some of the years which were found to be significant by means of a one-tailed test.

In all cases in this paper, when counting houses filtering down and up, we have neglected to specify what has happened in the rest of the houses. The other houses showed either no change, or the data were sufficiently ambiguous or lacking that no estimation of change could be made. Considering the large number of houses in each neighborhood (about 150), one can see that there were many houses which did not filter, or for which insufficient information was available to determine whether filtering did take place. Eighty or ninety percent of these other cases represented no change in occupancy, or no change in occupation.

A runs test was applied to the time series in each table by counting each year in which filtering down was greater than filtering up as a plus, and counting years when filtering up was greater as a minus. The sequences of pluses and minuses were grouped into runs. The null hypothesis is that the sequence is random. If there are too few runs or too many runs, the null hypothesis is rejected.[14] The null hypothesis could not be rejected at the 5 percent level of significance for either sequence.

One problem not indicated by the time series is whether there were many houses showing filtering up and only a few filtering down repeatedly, or whether a few houses filtered up repeatedly and many houses filtered down. Over the whole period, was the number of houses filtering down equal to or greater than the number of those filtering up? The study revealed that nine houses filtered up in Neighborhood One, whereas 41 filtered down. In Neighborhood Two, 11 houses filtered up and 43 filtered down. This result is significantly different from what one would expect if the probability of filtering down were equal to that of filtering up for the houses that filtered. This suggests that filtering did take place in the two neighborhoods.

Average price of housing for each neighborhood and for the city is shown in Table 9-3.[15] These data are based on sales transactions in the given years, and

Table 9-3
Average Prices of Housing in Kankakee, Illinois

Year	Neighborhood 1	Neighborhood 2	Total City
1918	4,000	4,450	3,319
1923	6,000	6,250	4,161
1925	8,000	6,500	4,175
1927	5,000	5,000	3,387
1929	9,600	12,500	9,600
1931	3,000	3,000	2,100
1933	1,000	7,200	5,875
1935	2,000	3,500	4,750
1937	4,750	4,666	4,000
1939	4,125	4,250	4,750
1941	3,100	6,425	5,000
1949	7,940	9,600	10,420
1954	10,440	8,300	12,500
1956	9,075	7,300	14,800
1958	6,050	6,450	15,260
1959	10,125	8,166	17,610
1961	6,450	12,283	11,270
1963	13,930	11,917	16,360
1969	13,200	11,283	28,320

Source: University of Illinois, Coordinated Science Laboratory, "Sales Prices of Houses in Kankakee, Illinois" (in progress).

may not actually represent the price of housing in the neighborhoods. Prices calculated in this way would depend upon which houses were sold and on the number sold in each year. The prices in this case have not been matched against the changes in occupancy in the directories. The price of housing in each neighborhood was generally above the average for the city until 1935, and is generally below the average for the city after this date. The prices show a generally rising trend, although there is some fluctuation which is probably due to the manner in which the prices were calculated.

From this evidence, it can be seen that the filtering process is quite gradual in its effects on a neighborhood. There were only a few years in which filtering down was enough greater than filtering up to have been statistically significant. In fact, filtering up seems to have occurred in some years. However, the number of houses filtering down over the whole period was significant, and other evidence in the full study corroborated that the filtering process did occur in the long run.[16]

The Webster Groves Case

The data on filtering in Webster Groves are shown in Table 9-4. In this case, an attempt was made to determine whether there was a difference in measured filtering depending on whether income of the households moving out was estimated from their last occupations or from their occupations when they first moved into the house. The first three columns show filtering when the occupation of the departing family is determined at the time of the move. This is identical to the way filtering was counted in the Kankakee case. As we indicated before, a householder's income could either rise or fall during his occupation of the house. He might be forced to move if his income should fall too much, because he couldn't keep up mortgage payments, maintenance costs, and property taxes. On the other hand, if his income should rise, he might prefer to move to a more expensive house. In either case, the new person moving into the house might have the same income as the occupant did when he first moved into the house. In such a case, it would be best not to consider that filtering up or down occurred.

The last three columns of Table 9-4 show the filtering count on the basis of the first occupation of the family moving out of a house. In only a few years does a difference show up. In neither case is there very much filtering down. In only one year, 1968, were we able to reject the null hypothesis that the probability of filtering down is equal to that of filtering up. Thus, the evidence bears out the common knowledge in the real estate market of St. Louis that Webster is a relatively stable community. It should serve as a good control group for further studies of declining neighborhoods.

Once again, a runs test was applied to the time series for each counting

Table 9-4
Filtering by Income in Webster Groves

	Count Based on Last Occupation of Out-mover			Count Based on First Occupation of Out-mover		
Year	Filtering Up	Filtering Down	Prob.[a]	Filtering Up	Filtering Down	Prob.[a]
1928	7	5	0.806	7	5	0.806
1930	5	5	0.623	5	5	0.623
1932	1	6	0.063	1	6	0.063
1934	8	9	0.498	8	9	0.498
1936	10	6	0.896	10	6	0.896
1938	11	5	0.961	11	5	0.961
1939	9	4	0.953	9	4	0.953
1941	9	7	0.774	8	8	0.599
1943	8	7	0.696	8	7	0.696
1946	10	9	0.675	12	7	0.915
1949	6	6	0.613	8	5	0.866
1953	6	9	0.304	5	9	0.212
1955	6	8	0.395	6	8	0.395
1957	6	6	0.613	6	8	0.395
1958	3	4	0.500	3	4	0.500
1959	4	4	0.636	3	4	0.500
1961	1	2	0.500	2	1	0.875
1962	2	4	0.344	2	3	0.499
1963	2	2	0.687	2	2	0.687
1965	3	7	0.172	4	7	0.274
1966	3	4	0.500	3	5	0.363
1967	2	3	0.499	2	4	0.344
1968	1	5	0.110	0	6	0.016*
1969	2	2	0.687	1	2	0.500

[a]This column shows the probability of drawing a random sample from a population in which $p = q = 0.5$ and finding a distribution equal to or more extreme than the one shown.
[b]Null hypothesis rejected at 5 per cent level.

method. Each year in which filtering down was greater than filtering up was symbolized by a plus. Each year in which filtering down was less than filtering up was symbolized by a minus. Years in which the number of houses filtering up was equal to the number filtering down was symbolized by a zero. A runs test on the grouping of pluses, minuses, and zeros was tried in order to determine whether there was clustering.[17] The null hypothesis is that the sequence is random. For neither sequence could the null hypothesis be rejected at the 5 percent level of significance. Nevertheless, there was only one instance of filtering up after 1949. Prior to 1949, filtering down occurred only in 1932 and

1934. If one eliminates the years in which no change occurred, there is statistically significant clustering. Thus, we may be observing the beginning of change within a community.

Considering occupation changes for each house over the period 1926 to 1969, the study revealed that 37 houses filtered up and 34 filtered down. This result is not significantly different from what one would expect if the probability of filtering down were equal to that of filtering up for the houses that filtered.

In the Kankakee case, particular neighborhoods were selected for study, whereas in the Webster case, a random sample of the whole community was taken. So far, the data reveal that there has been no significant filtering down in the community over the whole period studied. Thus, one more dimension that should be tested is whether filtering was significantly different by neighborhoods.

In order to test this proposition, Webster Groves was divided into four relatively homogeneous neighborhoods: (1) all of the blocks north and west of the Missouri Pacific railroad tracks and the Algonquin Golf Course; (2) all blocks south of a boundary starting at the eastern boundary of Webster and Lockwood, going west on Lockwood, north on Glenn Road, but excluding houses on both sides of Glenn Road, southwest along the Missouri-Pacific railroad tracks to the western boundary of Webster; (3) all blocks within an area bounded on the north by Newport, on the east by Bompart, on the south by Lockwood, and on the west by Glenn Road (except that houses on both sides of the street on Glenn Road are included in the area); and (4) all the rest of the blocks in the northeast portion of Webster not included in other neighborhoods.

Table 9-5 shows the number of houses filtering up and down in each of the above neighborhoods:

Table 9-5
Number of Houses Filtering by Neighborhood

	Neighborhoods			
	1	2	3	4
Filtering up	2	17	5	13
Filtering down	13	9	1	11

In only one neighborhood could we reject the null hypothesis that the probability of filtering up was equal to that of filtering down. In Neighborhood One, the probability of obtaining 13 or more houses filtering down, if the true probability were only .5, is about .003.

A file of the selling price of real estate in Webster Groves has been maintained for many years by the Roy Wenzlick Research Corporation. From their data, they have calculated a price index of single-family houses in the following way.[18] Taking only properties which have sold more than once for the time period considered, they find the ratio of each sale to the initial sale on each house. These ratios are then chain-linked, and a median for each year is determined. The medians represent the index of sales prices in each year. The advantage of the index is that it does not fluctuate with the style and kind of house put on the market each year. In fact, this was the difficulty with the averages we calculated for Kankakee.

In addition to utilizing the Wenzlick index for all single-family houses in Webster, we separated the group of properties in Neighborhood One and calculated a separate index for that neighborhood. Both indexes for the period 1939 to 1967 are shown in Table 9-6. Although there has been some tendency for prices to fade in Neighborhood One, they have continued to rebound up to the same rates of change as the properties for all of Webster Groves. In particular, it is important to note that Webster undertook an urban renewal project in Neighborhood One in 1961, which was completed in 1970. If there has been filtering in Neighborhood One, it has not been reflected in prices as yet. Furthermore, the Black population has been expanding in Neighborhood One, so that filtering may be offset by a pressure on prices caused by a shortage of housing for Blacks. Finally, the index for all of Webster Groves is smoothed by using a quarterly moving average, while there are fewer observations for Neighborhood One, in which such smoothing was not attempted.

Conclusions

The technique presented in this paper has been shown to be a useful way of measuring filtering. It has also shown that older neighborhoods do not filter in a regular way. Neighborhoods differ. The process itself has been shown to be slow, and not have any special time relation. One other comparison across neighborhoods can be made. A test of significance was run to determine if the proportion of houses filtering down over the whole time period in each neighborhood was significantly different from the others. At the .05 level of significance, the proportion of houses filtering down was not significantly different in the three neighborhoods. The same test was applied to the proportion of houses filtering up over the whole time period in each neighborhood. In this case, however, we found that the proportion of the sample filtering up in Webster Groves was significantly greater than that of either neighborhood in Kankakee. This leads to the interesting speculation that neighborhoods have similar tendencies for filtering down, but those that are stable tend to have a significantly greater amount of filtering up, balancing such change.

There will continue to be a need for collecting data to supplement the occupation information. The occupation data alone are insufficient to analyze the causes of filtering, although they are adequate for measuring the phenomenon. The present study should serve as a base for studies of other neighbor-

Table 9-6
Webster Groves, Selling Price Index,[a] 1939-1967, (1939 = 100)

Year	All Neighborhoods	Neighborhood One
1939	100	100
1940	100	90
1941	105	93
1942	114	100
1943	117	105
1944	136	115
1945	160	149
1946	214	200
1947	228	214
1948	248	206
1949	244	238
1950	252	252
1951	274	272
1952	281	269
1953	283	274
1954	288	267
1955	293	285
1956	293	292
1957	298	293
1958	300	272
1959	307	283
1960	314	288
1961	302	284
1962	305	306
1963	302	285
1964	300	282
1965	312	305
1966	321	306
1967	319	320

[a]Calculated from data in the files of Roy Wenzlick Research Corporation.

hoods. Comparison of maintenance expenditures, building code enforcement, and zoning regulations in a variety of communities should begin to reveal the causes behind why one neighborhood declines while others do not.

The strongest hypothesis that would be useful to test, however, would be whether filtering is itself a neighborhood effect—an externality. We know that like uses tend to occupy adjacent sites. Furthermore, we have a theory of the spread of slums that depends upon consumers wanting to live with other consumers of similar incomes and race.[19] Slums are created, in this theory, by the shifting of property to use for the poor, when the price as poor housing less the price as good housing can cover the cost of conversion to use by the poor. The conversion, however, moves across boundaries, so that location adjacent or near low income housing may be the determinant of how soon a neighborhood filters. To test such a hypothesis, the next steps in the study will be to analyze filtering by the same process, in two other suburban communities in St. Louis that are equally distant from the central business district, but are located differently with respect to the location of poor people in the metropolitan area.

Notes

1. Anthony Downs, "Housing the Urban Poor: The Economics of Various Strategies," AMERICAN ECONOMIC REVIEW (September 1969), pp. 646-651.

2. Homer Hoyt, THE STRUCTURE AND GROWTH OF RESIDENTIAL NEIGHBORHOODS IN AMERICAN CITIES (Washington, D.C.: U.S. Government Printing Office, 1939).

3. John B. Lansing, Charles Wade Clifton, and James N. Morgan, NEW HOMES AND POOR PEOPLE (Ann Arbor, Michigan: Institute for Social Research, The University of Michigan, 1969).

4. Herman P. Miller, INCOME OF THE AMERICAN PEOPLE (New York: John Wiley and Sons, 1950), and INCOME DISTRIBUTION IN THE UNITED STATES, 1960 Census Monograph (Washington, D.C.: U.S. Government Printing Office, 1966).

Other sources of occupational and industrial earnings data were as follows:

Paul H. Douglas, REAL WAGES IN THE UNITED STATES, 1890-1926 (Boston: Houghton Mifflin, 1930). Harry E. Jones, RAILROAD WAGES AND LABOR RELATIONS, 1900-1952: AN HISTORICAL SURVEY AND SUMMARY OF RESULTS (New York: Bureau of Information of the Eastern Railways, 1953). U.S. Bureau of the Census, HISTORICAL STATISTICS OF THE UNITED STATES, COLONIAL TIMES TO 1957 (Washington, D.C.: U.S. Government Printing Office, 1960). U.S. Bureau of Labor Statistics, EMPLOYMENT AND EARNINGS STATISTICS FOR THE UNITED STATES, 1909-1968 (Washington, D.C.: U.S. Government Printing Office, 1968). U.S. Bureau of Labor Statistics, HANDBOOK OF LABOR STATISTICS, 1969 (Washington, D.C.: U.S. Government Printing Office, 1969). U.S. Interstate Commerce Commission, WAGE STATISTICS OF CLASS 1 RAILROADS IN THE UNITED STATES (Washington, D.C.: U.S. Interstate Commerce Commission, 1957-60).

5. Herman P. Miller, INCOME DISTRIBUTION IN THE UNITED STATES, Chapter 4.

6. An explanation of the use of the binomial distribution can be found in

many introductory statistics books. For example, see Chapter 4 of Sidney Siegel, NONPARAMETRIC STATISTICS FOR THE BEHAVIORAL SCIENCES (New York: McGraw-Hill, 1956), or Chapter 5 of Samuel B. Richmond, STATISTICAL ANALYSIS (2d ed., New York: The Ronald Press, 1964).

7. There are two excellent sources for the historical material on Kankakee: Mary Jean Houde and John Klasey, OF THE PEOPLE: A POPULAR HISTORY OF KANKAKEE COUNTY (Chicago: The General Publishing Company, 1968), and Paul Wallace Gates, THE ILLINOIS CENTRAL RAILROAD AND ITS COLONIZATION WORK (Cambridge, Massachusetts: Harvard University Press, 1934).

8. Donald C. Guy, "An Analysis of A Filtering Hypothesis in Urban Housing Markets: An Empirical Test in Kankakee" (Unpublished Ph.D. dissertation, The University of Illinois, Urbana, Illinois, 1970), p. 79.

9. From an unpublished study of employment status in Kankakee in progress at the Co-ordinated Science Laboratory at the University of Illinois.

10. Harland Bartholomew and Associates, COMPREHENSIVE CITY PLAN, KANKAKEE, ILLINOIS (St. Louis, Missouri: The Author, 1949), p. 212.

11. The source of historical material on Webster Groves was William L. Thomas, HISTORY OF ST. LOUIS COUNTY MISSOURI (St. Louis, Missouri: The S.J. Clarke Publishing Company, 1911), 2 vols.

12. U.S. Bureau of the Census, U.S. CENSUS OF POPULATION AND HOUSING: 1960 CENSUS TRACTS, Final Report PHC(1)-131 (Washington, D.C.: U.S. Government Printing Office, 1962).

13. See newspaper items in the Moody Collection, The Missouri Historical Society, St. Louis, Missouri.

14. See Siegel, NONPARAMETRIC STATISTICS, pp. 52-58.

15. These prices were calculated from unpublished data collected by the Urban Planning Staff, Co-ordinated Science Laboratory, University of Illinois.

16. Donald C. Guy, AN ANALYSIS OF A FILTERING HYPOTHESIS.

17. W. Allen Wallis and Harry V. Roberts, STATISTICS: A NEW APPROACH (Glencoe, Illinois: The Free Press, 1956), pp. 571-572.

18. Roy Wenzlick, "As I See the Fluctuations in the Selling Prices of Single-Family Residences," THE REAL ESTATE ANALYST, vol. 21, no. 57 (December 1952), pp. 541-548.

19. Martin Bailey, "Note on the Economics of Residential Zoning and Urban Renewal," LAND ECONOMICS (August 1959), pp. 288-292.

10 The Effect of Aging and Income Transition on Neighborhood House Values*

(With Donald Phares and John Stevens)

Introduction

One typical view of neighborhood change is given in the Appraisal Institute's textbook of appraisal practice:

This, in a general way, is what happens to residential neighborhoods. They usually grow in desirability for a period after they are established, provided they command public favor, and are built up quite rapidly. They attain a peak of desirability, remain stable for a time, and then deteriorate in quality. Another way of stating it is there are three stages of neighborhood status—integration, equilibrium, and disintegration. If city growth and expansion are rapid, neighborhood change is likely to occur rapidly.[1]

The appraiser, of course, is describing the desirability of a neighborhood for family living. Changes in desirability would be reflected in housing values for the neighborhood. Appraisers appear to have a notion that the value of property in a neighborhood follows a cycle, increasing, reaching a peak, and declining. The mere passage of time, however, is not the sole determinant of the stage a neighborhood may have attained. Note that the quotation implies differences in the rate of change in different cities with different growth rates. On the other hand, one often sees comments that the reason for blight in the inner city is the age distribution of the housing stock.[2]

The purpose of this study is to show that a change in the income level of neighborhood residents is indeed manifest as decreased property values and that these changes are more likely to occur in neighborhoods adjacent to low-income areas, regardless of the age of the housing stock.

In an early article, Lowry questioned whether aging per se lead to deterioration.[3] With proper maintenance and improvements, the quality of any house could be maintained and it need not suffer economic obsolescence. Dwellings deteriorate because the income associated with the property declines. If the occupant is the owner, lower income means that less is available for maintenance and improvements. If he is a renter, less is available for rental payments so that the owner receives a decreased property income flow. In order to maintain a certain profit level, he makes less available for maintenance and improvements.

*Susan Edelstein, Steve Shortland, and Jim Wedemeier contributed yeomen efforts in the collection of the data. John Hand, Eugene Meehan, Richard F. Muth, and an unknown referee for LAND ECONOMICS provided many helpful comments on earlier drafts.

Declining property upkeep then is a rational adjustment to a decline in income associated with a particular property. Since property value is the discounted present value of earnings from property, its value will decline in response to lower occupant income.

Not only do we want to show that income transition is a more influential factor than age in determining property value but also that changing income is a result of the spatial contiguity of other neighborhoods in which income has already declined. It is quite common in real estate literature to emphasize that what happens to adjacent or nearby properties influences the desirability of a particular site.[4] Here we are hypothesizing that adjacent neighborhoods with a lower income or social status than a given neighborhood do indeed influence the trend of income and therefore property values in that neighborhood.

The test we have defined is an examination of the time trend in occupation-income ranks and property values in a variety of St. Louis neighborhoods located at varying distances from areas in which income has fallen. The study neighborhoods selected are the West End of St. Louis, Wellston, the Normandy School District, University City, and Webster Groves. Map 1 shows the location of each area. The age distribution of the housing stock is given in Table 10-1. The West End is the oldest study neighborhood, with 97 percent of its

Table 10-1
Age of Housing Stock and Income Changes of Households

Study Area	Percentage of Housing Built by Year[a]			Period of Change in Income	Income Change (Median Rank)	
	1939 or Earlier	1940-49	1950-60		From	To
West End	97	1	2	1952-55	8	7
				1955-56	7	6
				1958-59	6	5
				1960-61	5	4
Wellston	94	4	2	1934-36	4	5
				1938-53	5	6
				1959-61	6	5
				1961-69	5	4
University City	55	15	30	1965-66	9	8
				1966-67	8	7
Normandy	52	22	26	1966-67	7	6
Webster Groves	80	6	14	1966-67	9	10

[a]The data for Normandy, Webster Groves, Wellston, and the West End do not exactly coincide with the city or district limits of the study areas. The comparison is as exact as the use of entire census tracts will permit. In this table Webster Groves includes tracts 190, 191, 192 and 193, an area slightly smaller than the study area. Normandy includes tracts 122, 123, 136, 137, 138, 141, 142, and 143; Wellston, tracts 139 and 140; and the West End, tracts 5c, 5d and 5e.

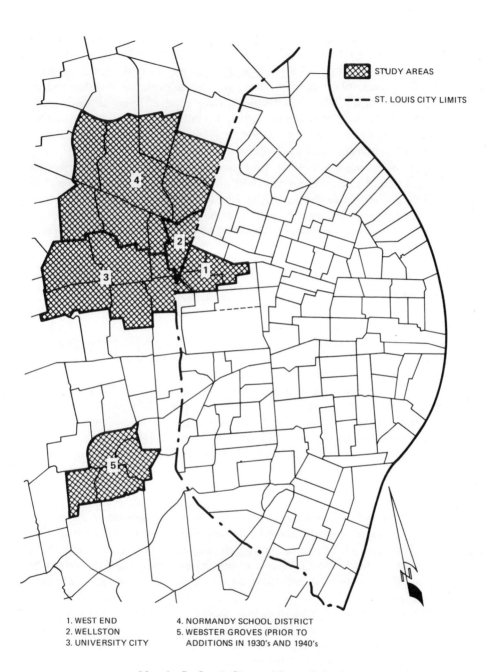

1. WEST END   4. NORMANDY SCHOOL DISTRICT
2. WELLSTON   5. WEBSTER GROVES (PRIOR TO
3. UNIVERSITY CITY   ADDITIONS IN 1930's AND 1940's

Map 1. St. Louis City and Inner Suburbs

residential structures built prior to 1939. Wellston, a suburb adjacent to the West End, is of about the same vintage. Actually, both areas were developed mainly prior to 1900. University City and Normandy, on the other hand, were not developed significantly until after 1900. In fact, almost half of their housing has been built since 1939. Both these suburbs are adjacent to Wellston and lie directly west of the West End. Webster Groves, however, began as a dormitory suburb as early as 1870. It was located on two railroad lines from downtown St. Louis, and many of its residents used the train to get to work in the city. Eighty percent of its housing stock was built prior to 1939.

If age were a more important determinant of housing transition than income or social change in contiguous neighborhoods, we would expect property values in Webster Groves to decline sooner than in University City. Our findings indicate this is not the case. As will be documented later in the text, property values in Webster Groves have increased both relatively and absolutely compared to University City and Normandy.

Data and Methodology

Obviously, to undertake the above test we need to compare time trends for both income and house values across neighborhoods. Comparison of the timing of income changes and the resultant value changes would be a direct and simple way to test our hypothesis about contiguity.

Census data do include estimates of median family income and median value of single-family houses. However, the information is only available decennially for 1940, 1950, 1960, and 1970. Since we are concerned with the timing of change, we need data that provide a more continuous time series. One source for the income information is the R.L. Polk Directories for St. Louis City and County.[5] While the Polk directories are not available for every year, they are available for every second or third year prior to 1960 and yearly since.

Although income information is not given explicitly, the occupation of the head of household is listed. Estimates of the income decile rank of the median earnings for these occupations can be derived from U.S. Census Bureau data for 1939, 1949, and 1959.[6] Accordingly, each occupation is assigned a decile rank from 1 to 10—the lowest 10 percent of wage earners being 1 and the highest 10 percent, 10. The rank for the nearest census year was used for each occupation in each year.

By converting occupations to income deciles, we avoid the problem of small changes in median income causing changes in the estimate of neighborhood income. Furthermore, income is only an approximation, and the decile rank seems a more reasonable estimate for a given occupation than a median-income figure. Since the income decile rank is based on median wages and salaries, we must assume that nonwage income is proportional to wage income.

Random samples of houses were selected from each neighborhood for the period from 1930 to the present, with the exception of University City, where the data were collected for the period 1949-1969. Using these data, we computed two measures of neighborhood change.[7] First, the median-income rank was computed for each neighborhood by year. Second, we determined the number of dwelling units that were occupied at the end of the study period by families with higher or lower income than at the beginning of the period.

To complete the analysis annual data on housing prices are required. Surprisingly, indices of actual sales prices by year for the sample neighborhoods were available.[8] Unfortunately, it was not possible to use these data because they were based on Federal Revenue Stamps affixed to property deed transactions. These stamps were no longer required after 1967, so that none of the series include the years since 1967. As will be shown in the next section, post-1967 value information is very important since much significant income transition occurred during this period. Therefore, it was necessary to use median rent and median value of single-family houses for each neighborhood from the Census of the years 1940, 1950, 1960, and 1970. Using these values, however, will prevent us from making any definitive statements concerning the timing of changes in value with respect to transition in income. Nevertheless, we are able to examine lags in income changes by moving from one neighborhood to an adjacent one since the income data are more continuous.

Estimates of Income and House Value Changes

In Table 10-2 we show the time period over which income data were collected in each study area, the total number of housing units sampled, and the number of units for which the income of the occupants increased or decreased. One possible test of the significance of income change is to treat the number of units exhibiting change as a binomial. That is, of those houses that showed a change in occupant's income, was the number of increases and decreases significantly different from what one would have expected if changes in either direction were equally likely? The probability of getting the changes indicated if the true probability of an increase or a decrease were both 0.5 is shown in the last column of Table 10-2.

While data for Webster Groves and Wellston were not significantly different from the distribution one would expect if the changes were equally likely, the West End, University City and Normandy all showed more decreases than would be expected. Thus, three of the neighborhoods showed significant declines over the entire study period. Significantly, they are contiguous areas (see Map 1). Also significant are the estimates of median-income rank in each year by neighborhood. Instead of showing a table with each year and its median, we indicate for each neighborhood the years between which the income rank

Table 10-2
Income Changes by Neighborhood

Study Area	Time Period	Housing Units in Sample	Lost Items (Units Changed to Commercial or Other Use)	Number of Units in Which Income:				Probability[a]
				Increased	Decreased	Did Not Change	Income Change Unknown	
West End	1930-1970	150	–	13	99	38[b]	–	0.000[c]
Wellston	1930-1970	189	3	26	35	13	112	0.134
University City	1949-1969	240	–	49	140	51	–	0.000[c]
Normandy	1930-1970	288	18	47	89	88	46	0.000[c]
Webster Groves	1926-1969	138	29	37	34	35	3	0.640

[a]The probability of drawing a random sample from a population in which the probability of an increase and a decrease is 0.50 and of finding a distribution equal to or more extreme than the one shown.

[b]Includes instances of both no change and change unknown.

[c]Null hypothesis ($H_0: P_x = P_y = 0.50$) rejected at 0.05 level of significance.

113

changed, the change in the median-income rank, and the age distribution of the housing stock. These are given in Table 10-1.

Decreases in income first occur—the medians decline—in the West End, then Wellston, University City, and finally Normandy. The first sign of downward transition is found in 1952-1955 in the West End, next followed Wellston in 1959-1961, then University City in 1965-1966, and finally Normandy in 1966-1967. There were periods in Wellston (1934-1936 and 1938-1953) and in Webster Groves (1966-1967) when income actually increased. Thus, the income transition that began in the area closest to the St. Louis central business district moved westerly from one neighborhood to the next adjacent neighborhood (refer to Map 1). University City and Normandy, both newer suburbs than Webster Groves, showed declines in income not found in Webster Groves. Webster Groves is considerably older than either University City or Normandy but is not contiguous to an area of income transition.

To show this transition phenomenon more explicitly we divided Normandy and University City into smaller subareas. In Normandy the division was made on the basis of major streets and the relative homogeneity of areas as shown in Map 2; in the case of University City it was made on the basis of elementary school districts, also a good approximation to homogeneity. This is shown in Map 3. For each of these subareas a count of houses in the sample in which income increased or decreased over the entire study period was made. The results showed that the northeast and southeast sectors of Normandy, the areas adjacent to change in University City and Wellston, showed statistically significant income transition (see Map 1). Other areas of the Normandy School District did not exhibit significant income decline. In University City the district showing change were those north of Olive Street, adjacent to Wellston and the West End. The rest of University City showed no change. Table 10-3 shows income change data by subarea within each study neighborhood. This further substantiates the impact of contiguity on income transition.

In University City we were fortunate to have additional data on the actual age of each house in the sample. These data also support the hypothesis that contiguity is more important than age. In the northern five school districts the average age of housing in the sample is 28 years. In the central three districts, and the southern two, the average age is 35 and 42 years, respectively! The five central and southern districts had not yet experienced income transition. The important point is that the average age of housing in the two major nontransition sections is 25-50% *greater* than in the transition area. The areas undergoing transition contain, on the average, smaller houses, 979 square feet compared to 1,201 and 1,092 square feet, with lower average value, $15,320 compared to $19,729 and $21,419, for the rest of University City.[9]

An additional facet of transition was revealed when data for Webster Groves were divided into the four homogeneous neighborhoods shown on Map 4. The northwest neighborhood had existed from the beginning of the community as a

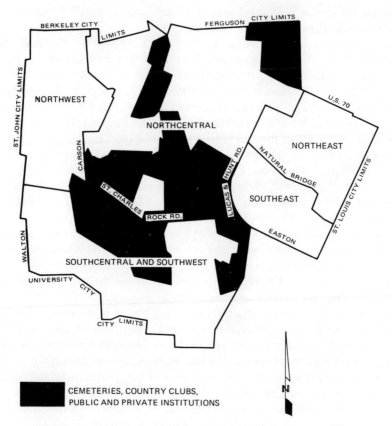

CEMETERIES, COUNTRY CLUBS,
PUBLIC AND PRIVATE INSTITUTIONS

Map 2. Normandy School District by Groups of Municipalities

black ghetto for servants of middle- and upper-income families in Webster Groves. In that neighborhood, the count of income change showed 13 houses occupied by families in which income decreased while only 2 showed an increase (see Table 10-3). The probability of obtaining at least 13 decreases out of 15, if the true probability of a decrease were 0.5 is 0.003; the change is statistically significant. Although these changes took place over the period from 1926 to 1969, no other area of Webster showed any statistically significant decrease. The barrier dividing this neighborhood from the rest of Webster Groves was a railroad track. What this may demonstrate is that small areas of isolated transition do not influence adjacent neighborhoods in a similar way to the massive change moving westward from the city of St. Louis. A further consideration is that this section of Webster Groves was an urban renewal area in which houses were rehabilitated

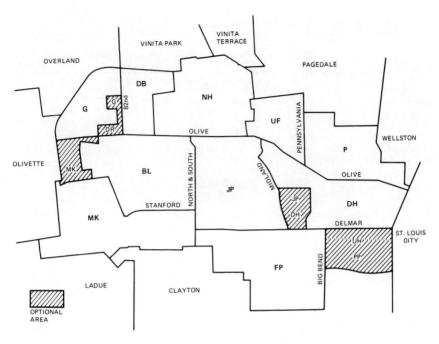

Map 3. University City by School Districts

selectively and in which demolition took place in order to build new housing and some industry.

Table 10-4 shows median value, gross rent, and contract rent for housing in each of the study areas for 1940, 1950, 1960, and 1970. In Table 10-5 these data are converted into relatives; the base is the median for the entire SMSA. The data in Table 10-5 indicate most dramatically that values in University City declined relative to those in Webster Groves and that values declined in the West End relative to those in Normandy. Prior to 1960 values were higher in University City than in Webster Groves and higher in the West End than in Normandy. Today the relative values in these areas are reversed. As mentioned before, these results would not be predicted if age rather than income were a major determinant of changes in value. All areas, however, including Webster Groves, were declining relative to the entire SMSA. In most areas the relative declines in rent and value were interrupted with an increase in 1950. Aging areas do tend to depreciate, but those not adjacent to areas of income transition do not decline as rapidly. In fact, rent in Webster Groves actually rose relative to the SMSA median.

Table 10-3
Income Changes by Neighborhood Subarea

Subarea	Filter Up	Filter Down	No Change or Change Unknown	Sample Size	Probability[a]
		WEBSTER GROVES			
Northwest	2	13	2	17	0.003[b]
South	17	9	21	47	0.962
Central	5	1	3	9	0.984
Northeast	13	11	9	33	0.729
Total	37	34	35	106	0.640
		NORMANDY			
Northeast	10	24	35	69	0.012[b]
Southeast	9	20	23	52	0.031[b]
North Central	13	22	32	67	0.088[c]
Northwest	4	6	12	22	0.377
South Central and Southwest	11	17	32	60	0.172
Total	47	89	134	270	0.000[b]
		UNIVERSITY CITY			
North	26	109	19	154	0.000[b]
Central	16	20	19	55	0.309
South	7	11	13	31	0.240
Total	49	140	51	240	0.000[b]

[a]The probability of drawing a random sample from a population in which $P_x = P_y = 0.50$ and of finding a distribution equal to or more extreme than the one shown (x = increase, y = decrease).

[b]Null hypothesis ($P_x = P_y = 0.50$) rejected at 0.05 level of significance.

[c]Null hypothesis ($P_x = P_y = 0.50$) rejected at 0.10 level of significance.

Conclusion

We have shown in this study that age is not the strong determinant of declining house values that many have suggested. Although age of housing is related to the value of property, the contiguity of neighborhoods experiencing income transition can change the trend of value in an adjacent neighborhood. Property does tend to deteriorate with age and indeed the transition of houses from higher to lower income families affects older housing first. Nevertheless, housing of similar age and value in certain parts of the metropolitan area not adjacent to massive transition in neighborhood income levels did not experience the same income change nor did it show a similar change in value and rent. Furthermore, those houses in University City for which occupants' income changed were newer than those houses in the same city that did not show such change. We have not suggested the way in which transition would move from one neighborhood to an adjacent one. More refined data are necessary to test any such hypotheses.[10]

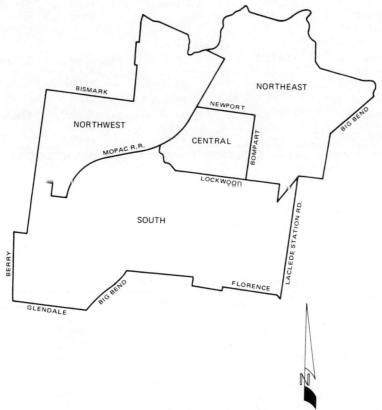

Map 4. City of Webster Groves by Neighborhoods

Table 10-4
Housing Value and Rent Characteristics, 1940-1970

Item	1940	1950	1960	1970
		West End		
Housing value	$4,371.00	$12,659.00	$12,800.00	$13,019.00
Gross rent	38.70	— [a]	74.00	—
Contract rent	35.52	50.02	—	75.00
		Wellston		
Housing value	$2,487.00	$5,642.00	$7,600.00	$7,669.00
Gross rent	24.35	—	69.00	—
Contract rent	17.38	29.00	—	66.00
		University City		
Housing value	$8,510.00	$15,000.00+[b]	$18,400.00	$18,600.00
Gross rent	50.41	—	107.00	—
Contract rent	45.66	55.23	96.00	116.00

Table 10-4 (cont)

		Normandy		
Housing value	$3,790.00	$9,826.00	$12,718.00	$14,083.00
Gross rent	31.80	–	86.50	–
Contract rent	24.53	41.58	–	110.47
		Webster Groves		
Housing value	$5,852.00	$13,728.00	$17,500.00	$20,100.00
Gross rent	41.52	–	102.00	–
Contract rent	33.46	44.12	83.00	127.00
		St. Louis Metropolitan Area		
Housing value	$3,856.00	$8,919.00	$12,900.00	$16,300.00
Gross rent	25.82	38.12	69.00	–
Contract rent	–	29.90	56.00	79.00

Source: Compiled from data in the CENSUS OF POPULATION AND HOUSING for 1940, 1950, 1960, and 1970.

aMeans not available.

bFalls in open-ended class $15,000 and over.

Table 10-5
Housing Value and Rent Relatives for Study Areas[a]

Item	1940	1950	1960	1970
		West End		
Housing value	113	142	99	80
Gross rent	150	–	107	–
Contract rent	–	167	–	95
		Wellston		
Housing value	64	63	59	47
Gross rent	94	–	100	–
Contract rent	–	97	–	84
		University City		
Housing value	221	168c	143	114
Gross rent	195	–	155	–
Contract rent	–	185	171	147
		Normandy		
Housing value	98	110	99	86
Gross rent	123	–	125	–
Contract rent	–	139	–	140
		Webster Groves		
Housing value	152	154	136	123
Gross rent	161	–	148	–
Contract rent	–	148	148	161

Source: Computed from data in Table 10-4.

aMedian for area as a percentage of the metropolitan area median.

bMeans not available.

cFalls in open-ended class of $15,000 and over.

Notes

1. American Institute of Real Estate Appraisers, THE APPRAISAL OF REAL ESTATE, 4th ed. (Chicago: American Institute of Real Estate Appraisers, 1964), p. 87.

2. Richard F. Muth, CITIES AND HOUSING (Chicago: The University of Chicago Press, 1969), p. 116.

3. Ira S. Lowry, "Filtering and Housing Standards: A Conceptual Analysis," LAND ECONOMICS, 36 (November 1960), pp. 362-370.

4. Otto A. Davis and Andrew B. Whinston, "The Economics of Urban Renewal," LAW AND CONTEMPORARY PROBLEMS, 26 (Winter 1961), pp. 100-110.

5. St. Louis City Directory and St. Louis County Directory (Detroit, Michigan: R.L. Polk, various years).

6. Herman P. Miller, INCOME DISTRIBUTION IN THE UNITED STATES (Washington, D.C.: U.S. Government Printing Office, 1966), pp. 96-97.

7. For a previous exposition of the techniques see, Donald Guy and Hugh O. Nourse, "The Filtering Process: The Webster Groves and Kankakee Cases," PAPERS AND PROCEEDINGS OF THE AMERICAN REAL ESTATE AND URBAN ECONOMICS ASSOCIATION, 5 (December 1970), pp. 33-49.

8. Ibid., Donald Phares, "Racial Change and Housing Values: Transition in an Inner Suburb," SOCIAL SCIENCE QUARTERLY, 51 (December 1971), pp. 560-573, and Joseph P. McKenna and Herbert Werner, "The Housing Market in Integrating Areas," THE ANNALS OF REGIONAL SCIENCE, 4 (December 1970), pp. 127-133.

9. Calculated from the Land and Real Estate Files of St. Louis County.

10. For one possible explanation see Martin J. Bailey, "Note on the Economics of Residential Zoning and Urban Renewal," LAND ECONOMICS, 35 (August 1959), pp. 288-292, Muth, op. cit., Chapter 6, and the Institute for Urban and Regional Studies, "Urban Decay in St. Louis," Washington University (March 1972), pp. 91-102.

11 Economic Analysis of Standard Quality Housing

Introduction

There are two responsibilities in research. One is to test propositions as we have been doing in the several studies in the previous chapters. The other is to formulate further hypotheses on the basis of the empirical tests. The material in this chapter falls in the category of generating further hypotheses.

It would appear easy to list the attributes of an adequate or standard quality house. Nevertheless, when the International Labor Office discussed the question, no specific attributes could be universally included:

A housing standard is defined—usually in terms of numbers of families per dwelling, standard of facilities per dwelling, and number and size of rooms needed for different families. These standards are largely arbitrary. They are based finally on what a particular investigator considers the needs of a family to be. . . .

There are no absolute and universal standards of housing, and it is impossible to develop such standards. For one thing, the specific requirements which need to be met in order to safeguard health and to assure a given standard of comfort vary greatly in different climates and locations; and, more important, what is regarded as an adequate standard of comfort will be determined according to local customs and local levels of income, and in response to long-term increases in real income and changes in taste and social conscience. It is easy to list the considerations that should be taken into account in determining housing standards. . . . To translate such a list of principles into terms of living space and facilities is a different matter. In fact, there are nearly as many housing standards as there are investigations into housing requirements.[1]

The standard of housing quality that can be obtained and maintained depends upon the amount of income the electorate is willing to redistribute in income or in housing to poor families. It is not dependent upon the standard set by a building or housing code. The purpose of this chapter is to show this in two ways. One will be a summary of the empirical evidence presented in previous chapters with additional facts with respect to public housing in St. Louis. The other will be the development of a model of the housing market that seems to fit the facts.

Public Housing

Property values of housing in a neighborhood appear to be more dependent on the socioeconomic character of the families living in the neighborhood than on the physical quality of the housing itself. The studies on the impact of public housing on neighborhood property values showed neither increases nor decreases. The families moving into public housing were similar to the families living in the surrounding housing units. Beyond this, however, there is an indication that the quality of public housing, when relatively new, did not have for the surrounding neighborhood social benefits that could be translated into increased property values.

A recent survey, however, has shown some benefits from public housing. Under fairly good controls groups of poor families from slum areas, some of whom moved into better housing and some of whom stayed in slum housing, were compared for differing rates of morbidity.[2] Better housing improved the health and school performance of children because they had fewer accidents and days of illness. These improvements were not found among persons over age 35.

At least up to 1967 the chief beneficiaries of public housing in St. Louis were both the residents and city government. The residents of public housing benefited by being able to occupy standard quality housing at a rent they could afford. The difference between costs and receipts to the public housing authority were made up by the federal government subsidy to pay interest and amortize the local housing authority debt established in constructing the project. The local government benefited to the extent that payments in lieu of taxes paid to the city by the local authority were greater than property tax revenues from the houses that the public housing families would have lived in had they not been in public housing.

One study of slum landlords found that their ability to bring a return on their investment was dependent upon their ability to select good tenants and keep them.[3] Some families through mismanagement or vandalism cause operating costs to be higher than if others with equal income should occupy the same units. One particular group frequently mentioned as causing an increase in public housing operating costs are welfare families with female head and four or five children.[4] Families causing these increased expenses will be called problem families. Private landlords must avoid such families if they are to break even, but public housing management cannot be so selective. These families must live somewhere. The difficulty is, however, that the proportion of such families in public housing has a tendency to increase over time. Because families must move out of public housing as their incomes rise above a certain level, problem families are likely to be left behind. Furthermore, out of each group entering public housing for the first time these problem families are most likely to remain, so that over time, the proportion of such families in projects increases. Since this will cause operating costs to rise, increased subsidies will be required to maintain the quality of public housing units.

This leads to a second financial problem. With income limits for families occupying public housing, family income and thus rents for public housing will not keep up with the inflation causing further increases in operating costs.[5] This causes additional pressure for increased subsidies to maintain the quality of public housing.

The St. Louis Housing Authority has found that it cannot provide housing to these families with the amount of the subsidy that they have been receiving. For the past several years the authority has received subsidies to cover part of operating expenses, in addition to the traditional debt service subsidy. In 1971 the St. Louis Housing Authority imposed a tenant selection rule to reduce the number of problem families in public housing. On November 9, 1972, the Authority Board of Commissioners voted formally to close its operation of conventional public housing.[6] The reason was that they have insufficient income from tenant rents, restricted to 20 percent of tenant adjusted gross income, to cover the operating expenses of their projects. The commissioners claimed that for all public housing units, $3,900,000 above the regular subsidy was needed. In response, the federal government has agreed to an additional subsidy of $1,600,000, but that amount, the commissioners say, would be insufficient. The mayor is trying to help keep the projects open by seeking ways that the city could take over some expenses, such as street maintenance, lighting, playground maintenance, staff salaries, and trash removal—expenses that the projects have had to pay previously.

Thus, the public housing experience indicates that there are at least two groups of poor, and that to house problem families requires larger subsidies than to house others who are equally unfortunate. Furthermore, the mere construction of good housing does not generate many external benefits to the rest of the community. Therefore, justification for the subsidy to these families rests on the willingness of the electorate to subsidize families to any standard arbitrarily set, such as those for public housing.

A Housing Market Model

Another way to make this point that housing need cannot be determined objectively, but is a result of the electorate's collective charity, is through an economic model of housing markets that appears to fit the evidence.

Consider a community or neighborhood with housing units of the same size and physical quality. There are five parallel streets of the same length. The streets are A, B, C, D, and E. There are neither vacant houses, nor families without houses. There are as many houses as families.

The first problem is to assign the families to houses. Half of the families have sufficient income to buy new housing; half do not. Furthermore, there are problem families among the poor. All other families will pay a premium to avoid the problem families. Unless an additional assumption is made, no solution to the problem is apparent. If, however, some nuisance, such as a railroad or polluting industry, should be located adjacent to street E, then the highest income families would pay the highest bid to be farthest from the nuisance, and would occupy street A, B, and one side of C. Alternatively, an attractive amenity adjacent to A street would cause the same result because the highest income families would pay the highest bid to be closest to the amenity. Lower income families would occupy the houses on streets C, D, and E. But there are two groups of these families—problem families who are difficult to house in "standard" housing without expensive subsidies, and other poor families. The latter pay a premium to avoid problem families and to locate adjacent to the higher income families. These families in a dynamic setting are the forerunners of the problem families. Expectations of such change would result in discounts on property values adjacent to poor families along C street.

Houses on streets A and B would be priced the same. Housing on the high-income side of street C would go for a discount on the prices P_h, of the houses on streets A and B. Housing on the low-income side of street C would go for a premium over the prices, P_1, of the houses on streets D and E. For an equilibrium to exist there would have to be no changes in population and income distribution. Furthermore, there would have to be no incentive to move. This would occur only if the prices, P_h, less a discount, d, on the high-income side of street C, were equal to the prices, P_1, plus a premium p, on the low-income side of street C. This would also indicate that P_h would have to be greater than P_1, and that the prices of housing on street C would lie between the other two prices.

Incentive for new construction occurs when the cost to build a new house is less than the present value of units in the current stock of housing. Thus, for there to be no incentive to add to the stock, the price of the standing units must be equal to or less than construction cost. Thus, equilibrium implies that P_h must be equal to or less than new construction cost. It follows that P_1 and the price on street C must be less than construction costs.

Even if all of the houses began in the same new physical condition, they would not remain in that condition long without subsidies from high-income families to low-income families. Families with lower income would simply not have sufficient income to maintain the houses in the same new quality as would the higher income families. If the houses were all owned by one owner, the same statement would be true. The rents received by the owner would be less than that necessary to compete with new housing, except on streets A and B.

The argument relies on the condition that the price, P_h, in equilibrium must be equal to the price of new units. Therefore, housing quality on streets C, D, E, and F would all deteriorate. They would deteriorate to a level that could be maintained with income from the property. It is possible that houses on F street could be very dilapidated depending upon the problem families living there.

The supply-and-demand model could be used to determine the impact of new immigrants to the community. If the new families would have high income, prices for high-income families would rise. This would force all prices up, and for an interim the high-income families must displace poor families on C or even D street. Poor families would have to double up. However, the increase in price P_h would give incentive to build new houses, and as long as the price remained higher than new construction costs, new additions would be added. A new equilibrium would occur when there was a house for everyone, the price of housing for high-income families was once again equal to construction cost, and C street was once again the boundary between the high-income and low-income families.

If the new families migrating to the community should be poor, prices on streets C, D, and E would rise. Initially, doubling up would occur, but with increases in P_1, prices on C street would rise, so that P_1 plus the premium was greater than prices on the high-income side of C street. Thus, there would be incentive to sell houses occupied by high-income families for use by poor families. As less housing became available to the higher income families, P_h would rise and new construction would occur. Equilibrium would occur when enough new housing had been built to accommodate all families, P_h had fallen to construction costs, and the number of streets occupied by poor families had expanded by as much as new housing had been built for upper income families.

A problem here is whether the border between high-income and low-income families would actually move unless a great deal of overcrowding among the poor occurred.

Nevertheless, the model needs an additional element to generate abandoned housing. In the above model abandoned housing simply would not occur. Each change in price would result in a maintenance adjustment, but someone would always occupy each structure. To generate abandoned housing, we need only introduce the public policy strategies presently current in the United States. The community imposes a building code standard that is higher than can be maintained by problem families without a subsidy. Furthermore, subsidies are made in kind through public housing or rent supplement.

With the introduction of the building code, houses on streets D, E, and F do not meet the code requirements. If the code is not enforced, not much would happen. There is an opportunity, however, for selective administrative discrimination against some landlords or owners. If the code is enforced, the housing would be abandoned. Incomes of the families would be insufficient to cover higher rents. If the families were homeowners, there would be insufficient income to pay for code requirements.

If the houses are abandoned because to maintain them at code would cause continuous losses, the houses available to the poor would be reduced. P_1 plus p, and P_1 wuld rise. Doubling up would occur, and the houses on C and B streets would be converted to use for the poor. Because the abandoned structures are in low-income neighborhoods, they are not profitable to purchase and use for new housing. Since the market would not reuse the property for housing, the demolition and reuse of the property depends upon other uses finding the site profitable. The reuse more than likely would require assembly of lots and perhaps even subsidy to obtain the appropriate scale so that new uses would be willing to locate near poor families. Previous land use decisions would suggest that the reuse may be a nuisance use. Our analysis in previous chapters, however, would not suggest that there would be any justification for the subsidy. Social benefits in reduced crime and fire hazards are illusory. The big question in the model is the reuse of the land. There is no economic rationale within the framework of the model suggesting a new use—except expansion of nuisance uses—such as truck terminals. If these uses are not expanding to occupy the abandoned sites, housing would remain abandoned.

The worst aspect of the model, however, is that as the poor occupy houses on streets B and C, after new construction has provided housing for the higher income families, maintenance deteriorates, and if owners must meet code standards, housing would be abandoned again—a continuous chewing up of housing resources. There is no static equilibrium. The model provides for continuous housing abandonment and pressure for new housing.

The continuous deterioration of the housing stock might be avoided if sufficient subsidy was provided to house the problem families. This subsidy either through public housing, rent supplements, or income redistribution would have to be so large that marginal families would resent the aid to problem families and have some incentive to become problem families themselves—or the redistribution would require a collective decision, and the aid would not be approved by voters. Token aid would achieve some improvement, but even those subsidized properties would succumb to abandonment, if the subsidy were insufficient to maintain the code standard.

Consider the usual market with continuous increases in the number of families, both poor and upper income. Housing is built continuously to meet the new demand. If prices are close to the construction cost of new housing, then poor families will occupy formerly higher income areas as fast as new housing is built. The imposition of the building code would cause abandonments, and P_1 and P_1 plus the premium would rise so that the number of houses occupied by higher income families would shift to lower income families faster than before the code. The rate of new construction would have to increase to bring the system back to equilibrium, so that P_h less the discount would be equal to P_1 plus the premium along the street bordering between the high- and low-income families.

The use of strict occupancy permits in conjunction with building code enforcement would not prevent the kind of deterioration forecast in the above analysis. It would prevent doubling up in neighborhoods occupied by poor families and would prevent some problem families from living in particular neighborhoods. Nevertheless, these families must live somewhere. Eventually, the law would be ignored and unenforced, as building code regulations often are, for otherwise, the occupancy permit allowing only a certain number of people in units of a particular size would cause houses to be abandoned, inasmuch as the only way they could be profitable would be with overcrowding.

So far we have not introduced the problem of racial segregation. If the races preferred to live apart, there would be discounts on house prices in integrated neighborhoods by families of both races. The evidence commonly cited, however, is that prices for blacks are higher than for whites. One model that fits the evidence is the model described by Martin Bailey.[7]

For reasons of prejudice, or anticipation of further changes, white families pay a discount for living in integrated neighborhoods. Blacks pay a premium. Given the geographic distribution of education expenditures, and that segregated black ghettos include poor and problem families, black families would be willing to pay a premium to avoid the central area of the ghetto.

Introduction of racial segregation would then create two streets of transition: one for racial transition, and one for income transition. Racial transition would occur as blacks newly moved into houses on street B, if we reconsider the original model with five streets A, B, C, D, and E. On the white side of B street, a discount from P_h would appear, and on the integrated side, a premium for black occupancy would appear. Integration would occur so long as the price blacks would pay for houses would be greater than that whites would pay for the same house. The difficulty is that blacks may not want to pay a premium after a certain proportion of blacks have arrived. Then neither blacks nor whites would seek housing in the neighborhood, prices would decline, and lower income families escaping abandoned housing would have a new area that they could afford.

As low-income families are pushed from their neighborhoods by the increase in abandoned housing, they push into integrated areas, where prices on housing are falling relative to other areas. Middle-income blacks, then, would be pushed to seek aggressively new areas to avoid poverty and problem families. The fact of segregation exacerbates the situation already created by subsidies that are lower than necessary to support the building code standards.

Conclusion

The way out of the circular and cumulative process is to forget the building code standard, establish it at the very minimum necessary to reduce fire hazards to others, or raise the subsidies so that every family can be housed at code standard. To implement the latter may require subsidies of differing amounts to families with the same income levels.

The above equilibrium model is built out of evidence from the empirical studies in this book. Nevertheless, it should be subjected to further testing. There are no easy answers. If these facts, assumptions, and speculations are true, there are no objective standards for planners to establish housing "needs."

Notes

1. International Labour Office, HOUSING AND EMPLOYMENT (Geneva: 1948), pp. 4, 9, cited in Robert Moore Fisher, TWENTY YEARS OF PUBLIC HOUSING (New York: Harper & Brothers, 1959), p. 29.

2. Daniel M. Wilner, Rosabelle Price Walkley, Thomas C. Pinkerton, and Matthew Taybeck, THE HOUSING ENVIRONMENT AND FAMILY LIFE (Baltimore, Md.: The Johns Hopkins Press, 1962).

3. Michael A. Stegman, HOUSING INVESTMENT IN THE INNER CITY: THE DYNAMICS OF DECLINE (Cambridge, Mass.: The M.I.T. Press, 1972), pp. 124-125.

4. Ibid., p. 272.

5. Frank deLeeuw, OPERATING COSTS IN PUBLIC HOUSING: A FINAN-CIAL CRISIS (Washington, D.C.: The Urban Institute, 1970) and C. Peter Rydell, FACTORS AFFECTING MAINTENANCE AND OPERATING COSTS IN FEDERAL PUBLIC HOUSING PROJECTS (New York: The New York City Rand Institute, December 1970).

6. ST. LOUIS POST DISPATCH, 9 November 1972.

7. Martin J. Bailey, "Note on the Economics of Residential Zoning and Urban Renewal," LAND ECONOMICS, vol. 35 (August 1959), pp. 288-292.

Index

Abandoned housing, causes, 125–126
  impact of building codes, 125–126
Age of housing, Normandy, 108
  University City, 108, 113
  Webster Groves, 108
  Wellston, 108
  West End, 108
Amenities, housing, 65
American Institute of Real Estate Appraisers, 64, 107
American Public Health Association, point system, 84
Annual contributions, public housing, 31, 39, 40
  Pruitt-Igoe, 45

Bailey, Martin J., 15, 60, 127
Beckmann, Martin, 79
Benefits, public housing, 3, 122
Blight, definition, 52–53
Building codes, impact on abandoned housing, 125–126
  impact on prices, 57, 125–126

Capital cost limitations, public housing, 31
Clifton, Charles W., 91, 93
Construction, criterion for, 76–78, 124
  impact of Pruitt-Igoe on, 46
  impact of public housing on, 36
  St. Louis, 46
Conversion of land use, criterion for, 77–78
Cost-benefit analysis, and redistribution of income, 29
Crime rate, Pruitt-Igoe, 47
Deterioration, effect of occupancy permits on, 126
Davis, Otto, 52
Downs, Anthony, 91
Durability, effect on changing land use, 64

Economic obsolescence, 5
External effects, of public housing, 3

Family income, public housing, 35
Federal income taxes, Pruitt-Igoe residents, 45–46
  public housing occupants, 34–35
Federal revenue stamp, in estimation of real estate prices, 8, 24n
  no longer required, 111
Filtering, definition, 93–94
  theory of, 123–127
Financing, liberal, effect on property value, 57–59

Friedman, Milton, 75, 76

Grebler, Leo, 4n
Gross rent income ratio, public housing, 33–34, 43, 44
  slum housing, 33, 43–44
Gross rent multiplier, defined, 77
  slum housing, 58–59
Guy, Donald, 91

Highways, effect on property value, 56
Housing values, Normandy, 118
  St. Louis Metropolitan Area, 118
  theory of, 64–70
  University City, 113, 117–118
  Webster Groves, 118
  Wellston, 117–118
  West End, 117–118
  (see also price index, prices, and property value)
Hoyt, Homer, 91
Hurd, Richard M., 63, 65

Immigration, effect on house prices, 124–125
Income distribution, effect on house prices, 65–70
Income elasticity, housing, 81
Income rank, estimates from occupation, problems, 92–93, 110
  Normandy, 108
  University City, 108
  Webster Groves, 108
  Wellston, 108
  West End, 108
International Labor Office, 121
Investment criteria, real estate, 76–78

Job access, and residential demand, 65

Koopmans, Tjallings, 79

Lansing, John B., 91, 93
Liberal Financing, effect on property values, 57–59
Lowry, Ira, 107

Maintenance Costs, problem families, 122
Marshall, Alfred, 63
Monroney, Senator A. S. Mike, 3
Morgan, James N., 91, 93
Muth, Richard F., 15, 55

Negative income tax, explained, 76

Neighborhood life cycle, 107

Occupancy permits, effect on deterioration, 126
Operating costs, mismanagement and vandalism, 122

Payments in lieu of taxes, versus property taxes, 36-38
  Pruitt-Igoe, 44-47
  public housing, 31, 40, 44-45
Phares, Donald, 107
Polk City Directories, 92, 110
Population, density of Pruitt-Igoe, 47-48
  Kankakee, 94
  Webster Groves, 95
Price index, and correlated errors, 22-23
  and depreciation, 18-19
  comparison of chain and regression methods, 23-26
  comparison of pollution versus control area, 71-73
  comparison of public housing versus control areas, 10-12
  construction of, 8-10, 15-19
  continual revision, 19
  illustration for three period case, 19-22
  Webster Groves, 101-103
  (see also housing values, prices, and property value)
Prices, and interdependency of demand, 79
  effect of immigration on, 124-125
  effect of income distribution on, 65-70
  Kankakee, 98
  (see also housing values, price index, and property value)
Problem families, and maintenance costs, 122
  subsidy, 122
Property value, and depreciation, 4
  and job access, 65
  defined, 36, 76-77
  determinants, 53-54
  effect of building codes on, 57, 125-126
  effect of highways on, 56
  effect of liberal financing on, 57-59
  effect of segregation on, 60, 123-127
  neighborhood effects on, 108
  (See also housing values, price index, and prices)
Public housing, compared to negative income tax, 86-87
  economic justification, 3
  function in government budget, 29-30
  operation, 30-31
  recent financial problems in St. Louis, 123
  transactions, 32

Quality of housing, 75-76, 121
  American Public Health Association point system, 84

Ratcliff, Richard U., 63
Real estate price index, (see price index)
Redistribution of income, and cost-benefit analysis, 29
  effect on house values, 80
Rehabilitation, hindrance to, 80-81
Rents, changes required to improve slum housing, 84-86
  Normandy, 118
  public housing, 30, 43-44
  St. Louis Metropolitan Area, 118
  University City, 117-118
  Webster Groves, 118
  Wellston, 117-118
  West End, 117-118
Residual receipts, 31
Roy Wenzlick Research Corporation, 101

Schaaf, A. H., 52, 84
Segregation, effect on property value, 60 123-127
Site value, defined, 4
  and small plots, 5
  as measure of net social return, 4
Slum housing, cost to improve, 84
  impact of economic growth on, 56
  operating costs, 38
  property taxes, 38, 40-41
  social cost, 52
  social theory of, 55
  tenant occupancy, 33, 43
  useful life, 38
Smith, Wallace F., 66
Social return (net), site value as measure of, 4
Stevens, John, 107
Stokes, Charles J., 55
Subsidy, dependent on electorate, 121-123
  effect on abandoned housing, 126
  effect on house prices, 126
  for problem families, 122
  Pruitt-Igoe, 45
  public housing, 3
Supply elasticity, housing, 81

Urban renewal, economic justification, 51-53

Vandalism, effect on operating costs, 122

Webster, Donald A., 53
Whinston, Andrew, 52

About the Author

Hugh O. Nourse graduated from Washington University (St. Louis) in 1955. While in college, he worked as an assistant research statistician for Stix Baer & Fuller. In 1959 he received the M.A. degree in economics from the University of Chicago. After two years as economist and Associate Editor of the *Real Estate Analyst*, Nourse returned to the University of Chicago, completing his Ph.D. in 1962. Since then, he has taught at Washington University (1962-64), the University of Illinois (1964-1970), and the University of Missouri at St. Louis, where he is currently Professor of Economics and Chairman of the Department of Economics. He is the author of *Regional Economics*, published in 1968.

Part 5